CW00509759

1,000,000 Books

are available to read at

---◇---

www.ForgottenBooks.com

---◇---

Read online
Download PDF
Purchase in print

ISBN 978-1-396-82147-9
PIBN 11364335

This book is a reproduction of an important historical work. Forgotten Books uses
state-of-the-art technology to digitally reconstruct the work, preserving the original format
whilst repairing imperfections present in the aged copy. In rare cases, an imperfection in
the original, such as a blemish or missing page, may be replicated in our edition. We do,
however, repair the vast majority of imperfections successfully; any imperfections that
remain are intentionally left to preserve the state of such historical works.

Forgotten Books is a registered trademark of FB &c Ltd.
Copyright © 2018 FB &c Ltd.
FB &c Ltd, Dalton House, 60 Windsor Avenue, London, SW19 2RR.
Company number 08720141. Registered in England and Wales.

For support please visit www.forgottenbooks.com

1 MONTH OF
FREE
READING

at

www.ForgottenBooks.com

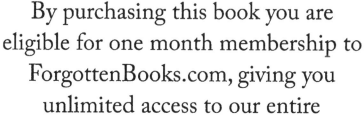

By purchasing this book you are eligible for one month membership to ForgottenBooks.com, giving you unlimited access to our entire collection of over 1,000,000 titles via our web site and mobile apps.

To claim your free month visit:

www.forgottenbooks.com/free1364335

* Offer is valid for 45 days from date of purchase. Terms and conditions apply.

English
Français
Deutsche
Italiano
Español
Português

www.forgottenbooks.com

Mythology Photography **Fiction**
Fishing Christianity **Art** Cooking
Essays Buddhism Freemasonry
Medicine **Biology** Music **Ancient
Egypt** Evolution Carpentry Physics
Dance Geology **Mathematics** Fitness
Shakespeare **Folklore** Yoga Marketing
Confidence Immortality Biographies
Poetry **Psychology** Witchcraft
Electronics Chemistry History **Law**
Accounting **Philosophy** Anthropology
Alchemy Drama Quantum Mechanics
Atheism Sexual Health **Ancient History**
Entrepreneurship Languages Sport
Paleontology Needlework Islam
Metaphysics Investment Archaeology
Parenting Statistics Criminology
Motivational

FOREIGN MISSIONS

OF THE

PROTESTANT CHURCHES . .

BY

STEPHEN L. BALDWIN, D.D.

NEW YORK: EATON· & MAINS
CINCINNATI: JENNINGS & PYE

4080

TWO COPIES RECEIVED,

Library of Congress,
Office of the

JUN 11 1900

Register of Copyrights.

a, 11175

May 3, 1900

SECOND COPY.

62888

Copyright by
EATON & MAINS,
1900.

EATON & MAINS PRESS,
150 Fifth Avenue, New York.

PREFACE

NO claim to striking originality is made for this volume, and it contains no profound philosophizing in regard to foreign missionary work. Its object is to present some of the principles which underlie the missionary work of Protestantism, to discriminate between conceptions of missions and missionary work that are true and those that are false, to consider the call and the qualifications of missionaries, briefly to treat of some of the methods by which the missionary work of the churches is managed from the home side and some that are employed in the work on the various fields, and to give brief outline summaries of the work of the numerous societies engaged in it but not to attempt at any length a detailed history of the work — which would require a much larger volume. Excellent works having such an object in view are already provided, and yet there may be room for one which will bring into as condensed form as possible a history of the work of Protestant missions generally.

A presentation is made of the different classes of fields occupied and of the general progress therein, and statistical tables are added to give a summarized view of some important items connected with the work of the Methodist Episcopal Church as well as of the whole Protestant missionary work.

Some of the books specially consulted were the *Cyclopedia of Missions*, edited by Dr. Edwin M. Bliss and published by Funk & Wagnalls, New York; Smith's *Short History of Christian Missions*, published by T. &. T. Clark, Edinburgh, together with various pamphlets and reports by different missionary societies. Where extended quotations are made it has been the purpose to give full credit to the authors.

It is hoped that the volume will be of use to students for the ministry, to those contemplating or who ought to be contemplating foreign missionary work, to all interested in the missionary cause, and that it may in its humble way further the advance of the kingdom of Christ in the earth by helping to increase the desire and the determination to fully obey the Saviour's command and as speedily as possible secure the preaching of the gospel, attended with its saving power, to all the inhabitants of the world.

STEPHEN L. BALDWIN.

New York, N. Y.

CONTENTS

CONTENTS

FOREIGN MISSIONS

OF THE

PROTESTANT CHURCHES

CHAPTER I

NATURE AND SCOPE OF CHRISTIAN MISSIONS

THE root idea of the word "missions" is that of sending. It comprehends the act of sending, the state of being sent, and the persons sent. The term "Christian Missions" includes the act of sending persons to preach the gospel of Christ, the persons thus sent, and also their operations.

Missions imply an authority sending, as well as persons sent, objects to be accomplished, and means to be used. For example, the United States sends a mission to Great Britain. The authority sending is the Government, representing the people of the United States. The person sent is a trusted citizen of the commonwealth, who is made for this purpose the representative of the Government and the nation. The object to be accomplished is the negotiation of a treaty to secure certain rights and privileges. The means to be used are argument, persuasion, and the concession of certain rights and privileges in return for those to be secured.

The authority in Christian Missions is the Lord Jesus Christ. He is the Head of the kingdom whose interests these missions are intended to promote. When he instituted them he affirmed: "All power is given unto me in heaven and in earth;" or, as the Revised Version renders it, "All authority hath been given unto me in heaven and on earth." Paul desired the Ephesian Christians to know "what is the exceeding greatness of his power to us-ward who believe, according to the working of his mighty power, which he wrought in Christ, when he raised him from the dead; and set him at his own right hand in the heavenly places, far above all principality, and power, and might, and dominion, and every name that is named, not only in this world, but also in that which is to come; and hath put all things under his feet, and gave him to be the head over all things to the church, which is his body, the fullness of him that filleth all in all." Eph. i, 19-23.

The persons commissioned are, in a general sense, all disciples. "The Spirit and the bride say, Come; and let him that heareth say, Come." Every one who has heard the Master's voice is delegated to make known the gracious invitation of divine mercy. So we read in the very earliest history of the Christian Church, when the disciples were widely scattered by cruel persecution, "Therefore they that were scattered abroad went every where preaching the word."

In this sense every disciple is an ambassador of Christ to his fellow men, but in a more special sense the ministry is set apart for this work. The old queries of the great Apostle to the Gentiles have lost none of their force or pertinency: "How shall they believe in him of whom they have not heard? and how shall they hear without a preacher? and how shall they preach except they be sent?" The sinful race must be brought to trust in Him who gave himself for them; but in order to trust in him it is necessary that they should know him, and become acquainted with the blessing he has to bestow and the terms he has to offer. That they may come to this knowledge it is necessary that the proclamation of this divine Saviour and the terms of his mercy be clearly and definitely made universally known. That this may be authoritatively done there must be persons duly authorized and regularly commissioned to go forth and make them known. So, from the beginning, chosen men, called of God, have been solemnly set apart to this work; consecrating their lives to this glorious service, a work that indeed

> " might fill an angel's heart,
> And filled a Saviour's hands."

This is not the place to discuss the call and qualifications of the Christian ministry. It is only referred to here as necessary to the complete view of our subject. Special calls to and qualifications for specific missionary work will come under review hereafter. We are now to consider the work committed to Christ's ambassadors.

It is very tersely and definitely stated in Christ's own words, as given by Mark (xvi, 15): "Go ye into all the world, and preach the gospel to every creature." It contemplates making known the gospel provisions of salvation to every human being. This is the simple yet grand and majestic work committed to the hands of the Christian ministry. It will be seen that it leaves little room for making a distinction between home and foreign missions. The mission of Christ's ambassadors is one. If we preach to sinners in America it is because they are included in "all the world" and "every creature" to whom we are sent. The same authority which permits us to preach to them binds us to preach to the dwellers on the mountain sides of China, to the tribes of interior Africa, and to the inhabitants of the isles of the sea.

Matthew (xxviii, 19, 20) gives a fuller form of the Great Commission in these words: "Go ye therefore, and teach all nations, baptizing them in the name of the Father, and of the Son, and of the Holy Ghost; teaching them to observe all things whatsoever I have commanded you." Revised Version: "Go ye therefore, and make disciples of all the nations, baptizing them into the name of the Father and of the Son and of the Holy Ghost: teaching them to observe all things whatsoever I commanded you."

No embassy ever had its work more clearly defined. "Go ye into all the world." That disposes of the idea sometimes advanced that we are to spread the gospel by letting all the world come to us. We are told, "This is the great gathering place of all the nations; here are Swedes and Germans and Italians and Chinese and Japanese, let us stay here and evangelize our own country; we can convert Germans and Scandinavians and Chinese faster here than we can in their native lands." But in the marching orders of Christianity there is no commission nor permission to "stay here." The first word in our charter is "Go!" This is the keynote of Christianity, and it sounds at once in the heart of every new-born child of God.

> "The arms of love that compass me
> Would all mankind embrace."

And, although he goes first to those nearest to him, the impulse to go and the object in going can never be satisfied until those who dwell in the uttermost parts of the earth are reached. Though the opposition in our churches to foreign missions has much weakened there is still in many quarters a marked indifference to them, to say the least; and the question is sometimes asked, as if there were some ponderous significance in it: "Were not the disciples commanded to begin at Jerusalem?" Certainly they were; but the emphasis in that instruction is not on the word *Jerusalem*. There must be some place to start, and the best place for that purpose is always just where one is. The disciples were in Jerusalem, and that was the place for them to begin. The purport of the divine direction was, "Take up the work where you are, and then go on as God opens the way." But the Master took good care that the disciples should not stay in Jerusalem, even using persecution to make an intensely missionary church of them; sending them "every where preaching the word."

"The field is the world." The whole field must be worked. Every foot of the territory must be subdued to its rightful Master. How many shall be employed here and how many there must be decided by sanctified Christian generalship; but the whole field must be kept in view, and every local movement ought to have reference to the enterprise as a whole and to the final result. Whether Grant should go down through the Wilderness, or lay siege to Richmond, or attack Petersburg; whether Sherman should help in these operations, or should rather go sweeping down to the Gulf and then turn northward to crush the enemy between his forces and those of Grant—these were questions of expediency to be decided in view of the final result, the entire conquest of the whole field for the Union. So it may be a question of expediency how many men shall be sent to China, how many to Japan, how many to Africa, this year. But that any man shall say, "I have a commission to preach to a fashionable congregation in Boston, or Philadelphia, or Chicago, and I do not acknowledge any responsibility beyond this," is not permissible. There is no such commission. The commission is to go "into all the world, and preach the gospel to every creature." In what particular portion of the field any minister shall just now labor is a question to be decided by providential indications, by divinely sent impressions, and by the use of sanctified common sense; but let no ambassador of Christ try to shirk the obligation imposed upon him by his commission. Nay, let no one of them be willing that a single word shall be omitted from his glorious credential!

In this field the work to be done is to "preach the gospel." Men are rebels to be brought into allegiance; sinners to be saved. There is only one authority competent to settle the terms, and this authority has settled them. The business of his ambassadors is to proclaim those terms. They are very simple. The words of Paul to Timothy and the words of Paul and Silas to the Philippian jailer cover them: "Christ Jesus came into the world to save sinners." "Believe on the Lord Jesus Christ, and thou shalt be saved."

To make known the coming and the sacrifice of Christ, its object, and the way by which that object may be secured, this is the clearly defined work of Christ's ambassadors. A plainer or more simple commission no mortal ever held. A grander or sublimer one was never entrusted to archangel. To the

blood-stained millions of earth this message comes:
You have sinned, and God's wrath is evermore
against sin. You cannot save yourselves. But God,
whom you have offended, still loves you, and he himself has planned the means of your redemption.
His only Son has suffered for you, and if you will
give yourselves to him he will take your case into his
own hands, forgive all your past sins, and purify
your hearts so that you can render acceptable service to your King. This, then, is the message which
is to be taken to all men. There must be no toning
down, no compromise.

No distinction as to these plain terms of salvation can be made between sinners on Fifth Avenue
and sinners at the Five Points. If the former do
not like the classification into which this throws
them their best course is to get out of it by giving
their hearts to Christ. Paul had no terms to offer
to the cultured Athenians different from those given
to the rude islanders of Melita. Our work would
be very much more complicated if we were com-
pelled to adapt the conditions of salvation to the
various classes of men we are to meet, but as it is
we have perfectly clear sailing. There is no danger of mistake except when we depart from the
terms of the commission. When we preach to men
as sinners, when we hold up Christ before them as
the Saviour, when we tell that the salvation he has
provided is to be realized by immediately accepting
his terms and giving him the full trust of their

hearts we are in no danger of making a mistake. It is as safe to make this proclamation in Japan or Zululand as in Boston, and as safe to make it in Boston as in any heathen land. If we go to philosophizing on theories of the atonement it is quite possible we may bewilder our hearers and find ourselves bewildered; if we spend our time in attempts to justify all the ways of God to man we may involve both ourselves and our hearers in serious difficulty; but if we are loyal to our commission, and proclaim everywhere the divine terms of salvation on the authority of him whose ambassadors we are, we will be upon firm ground, sure of his approval and of his blessing.

But not only are Christ's ambassadors authorized to proclaim the terms of salvation. They are commanded to make disciples of all nations, "Baptizing them in the name of the Father, and of the Son, and of the Holy Ghost." But they are not to be baptized in order to make disciples of them, as some even in our day erroneously teach. Christ never attributed any saving power to the water of baptism. When some of the members of the church militant, of whom ecclesiastical history tells us, marched into a country and drove the inhabitants by thousands to baptism they went far beyond the commission. Even in regard to the ceremony of the older dispensation the apostle said, "Neither is that circumcision which is outward in the flesh;" but "circumcision is that of the heart, in the spirit, and not in the letter." If not even a true Jew could be made by circumcision certainly a true Christian cannot be made by baptism.

All the subjects of this kingdom are voluntary ones. As Philip said to the eunuch who desired baptism so all true ambassadors of Christ say to-day to every applicant, "If thou believest with all thine heart thou mayest." We have no commission to baptize heathen or unbelieving sinners of any other kind. We are commissioned to proclaim the terms of salvation and urge their acceptance. When those terms have been accepted, and the persons to whom we preach have yielded their hearts to Christ, then we are authorized to bestow the outward sign of the inward grace; allowing them to make public profession of what they have experienced. We are not to baptize them to make disciples, but because they are disciples. We do not affix a seal to a deed in order to make the deed, but to show that it is made. This work of discipling is to go on until we shall have made "disciples of all the nations." Nothing less than this can fulfill the terms of our commission.

But a most important part of the work included in the commission remains still to be considered: "Teaching them to observe all things whatsoever I have commanded you." Not only are men to be turned from their sinful lives and led to make full surrender to Christ, but they are to be trained in all that belongs to citizenship in his kingdom;

in obedience of heart, of spirit, of life; in the growth
and development of Christian character. Just as we
say of the freedman, "It is not enough that he is a
citizen; he must be instructed in the Constitution
and laws of his country and in the duties of citizenship," so we may say of the newly admitted
citizens of Christ's kingdom; and the commission
makes provision for this very necessary and important work. Those who are brought out of rebellion
into allegiance must be instructed, and that which
is to be the subject-matter of instruction is "all
things" which Christ has commanded. The work of
indoctrination in the great cardinal truths of the
gospel and in the duties of the Christian life must
be thoroughly performed if we are true to the terms
of our commission. It is not enough that converts
are made, though a loose phraseology is often used
that seems to imply that the work is all done when a
man is converted; but whenever a babe is born
there is a child to be trained, and in every mission
station the addition of converts implies an immense
after-work to be done in training these babes in
Christ in all that belongs to the commandments of
their divine Master. This may be a far more difficult and troublesome work than the simple proclamation of the gospel, but it is not therefore to be
neglected or slighted. Missionaries have been
known ere this who delighted to roam over the
country preaching the gospel and who much pre-
ferred that all the details of church organization,

the oversight and training of the converts in all that pertains to godliness, should be left to other hands. But we are never to forget that it is as much a part of our commission to teach the disciples as it is to get them to be disciples.

Our consideration of Christian Missions has thus brought before us, 1. The authority sending: the Lord Jesus Christ. 2. The persons sent: all his disciples, and in a special sense the ministers of his word. 3. The object to be accomplished: the bringing of all people into allegiance. 4. The means to be used: the preaching of the gospel, and instruction and training in the teachings of Christ. His ambassadors, engaged in this great work, are inspired by the gracious promise of his presence with them "alway, even unto the end of the world."

This presents Christianity to us as an essentially aggressive institution whose object is nothing less than the conquest of the whole world for Christ. It leaves no debatable ground. Loyalty to Christ requires acceptance of the commission and obedience to it. Christianity does not accept a position as one of the religions of the world. The proposition to admit Jesus as one of the gods of the Roman pantheon could not be accepted; when Jesus appeared there it was the signal for all the heathen gods to leave. No true servant of Christ can consent to place his Master alongside of Socrates, of Zoroaster, of Buddha, or of Confucius, and say, "I give homage to all;" he must rather say, "I bow before Christ as the all in all." All of truth, in any realm of thought, that has been given to any sage or philosopher let us gladly acknowledge; but when the way of salvation is asked for "there is but one name given among men." There is but one religion, and that is for the whole race; and its one Head is the King before whom every knee must bow, and whom every tongue must confess. Any man who looks upon Christianity as one of the redemptive agencies for mankind—a civilizing and elevating power among others—has a radically wrong conception. It claims to be the divinely ordained system for the salvation of the race. It must be taken to all the world. It must be preached to every creature. It must conquer individual hearts, and by making these heart conquests disciple all the nations.

It is in the nature of things that such a system must be aggressive. A religion intended for all mankind, adapted to all mankind, claiming the homage of every human being, putting forth as its object at the very outset the discipling of all nations —such a religion cannot be otherwise than aggressive. Its claims are in conflict with those of all other religions the world has known. It boldly proclaims that salvation is not to be found in any of them. It tells not of *a* saviour, but of the one only Saviour; and it insists that he must reign until he has put all things under his feet. This is the true "light of Asia," because it is "the light which

lighteth every man that cometh into the world."
Inasmuch as "men love darkness rather than light,"
there are those in the midst of Christianity's sun-
shine who talk of the "great teachers," Plato and
Socrates and Zoroaster and Jesus; who dwell on the
"beautiful teachings" of these great teachers, to
whom they yield almost if not quite equal homage;
who compliment Buddhism and Brahmanism as
being well adapted to the people among whom those
religions flourish; men who boast of their liberality,
and of having escaped from all bonds of superstitious reverence, but who do not seem to compre-
hend that there is a world of rebels against God to
be dealt with, and that God himself has prescribed
the terms on which these rebels may be pardoned
and become members of his own household.

We are called to a very serious and earnest work.
We have no time to spend in passing compliments
on false systems of religion; in throwing the light
of Christianity around a form of godless heathenism
until we get some partially sensible people to believe that it is almost as good as Christianity itself.
Christianity is everything, for this fallen race, or
nothing. If it be not what it professes to be—the
one way of salvation for all men—it is a delusion
and an imposture. Every true minister of Christ is
necessarily a missionary. Inwrought in his soul
is the conviction that the world needs Christ; that
Christ is provided for the world; that the world
may receive him; and this conviction enables him

to proclaim in all sincerity the great truth of the gospel—that Christ Jesus came into the world to save sinners.

Another thought is connected incidentally with the subject of this chapter. This review of the nature and scope of Christian Missions gives us the true basis of missionary work; namely, obedience to the command of Christ our King. It is irrelevant to inquire how many of the heathen may possibly be saved without a personal knowledge of Christ. We are not responsible for the dead heathen, except in so far as we may have allowed them to die in heathenism when we might have taken the light of the gospel to them. It is not necessary that we should settle what their condition is. It is enough for every loyal subject to know that his commission reads, "Go—preach—make disciples." Is not this divine command the very best authority and the grandest inspiration for the work? But we are asked, Does not the Master say, "He that believeth and is baptized shall be saved; and he that believeth not shall be damned"? Yes; but nobody construes this language to imply that literally everyone who does not believe personally on Christ must be eternally lost. No one in these days applies it to infants dying in infancy. Sanctified common-sense interprets it, "of those to whom this message comes, and who are capable of comprehending it, he that believeth and is baptized shall be saved."

Ministers of Christ ought to take the broadest

and noblest view of their grand vocation. It should not be considered a commission to take charge of some well-established church in a pleasant and cultured community. That will have to be done by some, as a part of the great work, but no earnest servant of God should be anxious to do it. It is a useful work to take a beautiful garden, in which are elegant flowers and luscious fruits, and till it, pruning a little here and there, adding to its decorations, developing more new varieties of beautiful flowers, trimming the hedges, and improving its appearance, without much real addition to its usefulness, but it is a grander, a nobler, a more soul-inspiring work to go into the midst of a wilderness and make a garden there. To see the changes which come over it as chaos and disorder are gradually resolved into forms of beauty; as barrenness and bleakness give place to fertility and fruitfulness. Considering the Master we serve, the work he gives us to do, the object he designs to accomplish, which seems the more desirable: to have it written, "He came to this church. It had four-hundred and twenty-five members; he received seventy-five more; he weeded out fifty names that ought not to have been on the church rolls; he left us with four hundred and fifty. He reduced the debt from ten thousand to five thousand dollars; he was a good pastor and a faithful preacher;" or to have it written, as it was of the noble missionary to one of the New Hebrides islands, "When he came there was not one Christian; when he left there was not one heathen"? It is not intended to intimate that all ministers should become missionaries to the heathen, but to say, "Covet earnestly the best gifts." Seek to do the most possible for Christ your Lord. Be glad of the call that takes you to the front; that honors you with the order to advance into the enemy's country for your Master. Hold yourself in readiness for the Master's call. The spirit of full surrender, of deep and thorough consecration of yourself and all your powers, which will enable you to do this, will be your best qualification for the Master's work—whether that work is to be done at home or abroad.

CHAPTER II

FALSE AND TRUE CONCEPTIONS OF MISSIONS AND MISSIONARY WORK

IT is important at the outset to get a true conception of missionary work, especially as to its real place in the activities of the Christian Church. We shall be greatly assisted in forming a right conception by examining various false conceptions which are entertained, and are widely prevalent, in regard to this matter.

It is a very common error to look upon missionary work as simply one of the benevolent agencies of the times. The place it occupies in many minds may be represented in this way: In the community are many children who are left orphans and who are in circumstances of great need. It is the dictate of the human heart to care for them and to provide for their education so as to fit them for the duties of life, therefore an orphan asylum is instituted where these unfortunate ones can be received, where kind care will be given them, and every effort will be made to fit them to become useful members of society.

Again, we find in the community many deaf mutes. Their inability to hear and speak puts them to disadvantage in many respects and shuts them out from instruction in the ordinary schools. They must have special institutions and peculiar methods of education. Humanity dictates that special provision should be made for them, and therefore institutions are organized where this unfortunate class can receive the instruction adapted to their peculiar necessities.

Here are also large numbers of blind people. Deprivation of sight is a great calamity to them. Benevolence says, "Help them in their trouble; open institutions to receive them. They cannot be taught to read our common books; make books for them with raised letters, so that fingers may do the work of eyes, and they may thus have opened to them the Holy Scriptures and books of useful knowledge." Hence arise our institutions for the blind.

Now, the conception which many people entertain of mission work is right along on this line. Here is a class of unfortunate people who have been taught to worship idols and whose minds are darkened by ignorance and gross superstitions. They are in a sad and pitiable condition. It is the dictate of benevolence to send to them the light of Christianity. There ought to be an organized effort for their enlightenment and salvation, and it is well for all humane men to give their countenance and support to such a movement.

The effect of such a view of mission work upon those holding it is not difficult of discovery. The man who holds it, when applied to for help for an orphan asylum, or for an institution for the blind or for the deaf and dumb, says to himself, "How much can I spare for this benevolence?" and he makes a donation—larger or smaller according to various circumstances which combine to affect his decision. To his mind, the appeal for help in carrying on mission work presents very much the same aspect: it is simply one cry amid innumerable others for help; and it seems a far-away and indistinct cry compared with some of those that are near at hand, and which appear to him very urgent. The work of missions therefore takes its place with him among the other benevolences; he gives to it a greater or less sum, with more or less heartiness, just as to any other of the benevolences upon which he bestows his aid. That this is a radically wrong conception will clearly appear when we come to contrast it with the right conception.

Another view quite commonly taken of missionary work is that which regards it as a civilizing and educating agency. There are many men who are profoundly impressed with the great blessings of civilization. They regard nations which are in a barbaric condition with intense pity; and nations that are lacking in any of the elements of the best and highest civilization excite their commiseration just in proportion to their deficiency in this respect. Then, too, anything that adds to the general sum of human knowledge—anything that throws light on the history, the geography, the philosophy of foreign countries, or makes known the peculiar customs and habits of their people—is regarded with great favor. The establishment of schools for instruction in Western learning is welcomed by such persons. They favor exploration societies, which seek to dig up from the earth the ruins of ancient cities and bring to light the hidden things of ancient history. They look with great favor upon such a movement as that of Stanley's, to establish a great free state in Central Africa to be a center of enlightenment and of healthful influence to all the surrounding tribes. Anything which will help the adjustment of favorable moral conditions meets with their philanthropic welcome.

Now, there are not wanting many who view the missionary enterprise simply in the light of a civilizing and educating agency, and who support it precisely on the same ground on which they support any other philanthropic agency which proposes to diffuse the light and blessings of civilization among the uncivilized, or to add to human knowledge by the discoveries it may make and of which it will give due report. This also is a low, insufficient, and radically wrong conception of the work of missions.

Another false conception of mission work is that which considers it an agency or department in the work of the Church. In the minds of many, certain things are looked upon as incidental to the operations of the Church—auxiliary agencies, to be made use of in carrying on its work. For instance, the Sunday-school is regarded as such an agency; a very desirable and excellent institution for bringing Scripture instruction to the minds of children and youth. It was right for the Church to institute it, but there is no divine obligation to continue it. It is a question of expediency, to be decided altogether by its demonstrated usefulness.

So with the work of education. It is very desirable to provide means of mental training within the Church—especially to make adequate provision for instruction in the higher branches of learning under Christian auspices. The Church has taken up this work, and has prosecuted it with greater or less vigor according to the means at its command and the urgency of the demand at different times and in different places. It is a work that may be done, or, if circumstances are unfavorable, may be left undone. It is legitimately within the province of the Church, but it is not so essential that the Church may not exist without it.

Now, the view of missionary work which we are considering puts it in the same category with these other agencies; and this is just the place it occupies in the minds of many Christian people. To their thinking, the Church is looking about to see what benevolent and philanthropic work it can engage in. Seeing the necessities of children and youth, it opens Sunday-schools, and organizes a Sunday-school Union. Seeing the desirability of higher education under Christian auspices, it seeks to provide the same for its youth and to give such assistance as is needed in its attainment, and organizes an Education Society. Seeing the darkened condition of the heathen world, the superstition and ignorance still prevailing in many Christian countries, the spiritual degradation of great masses of people in the cities and in frontier regions, it institutes missionary work and organizes a Missionary Society. So this work of the Church simply takes its place in their minds alongside of Sunday-school, educational, and other benevolent agencies. This, too, is a radically wrong conception; and wherever it prevails it is an obstacle to a proper appreciation of the true position of missionary work in the Church of Christ.

Closely allied to these wrong conceptions of the relations of missionary work to the Church are false conceptions in regard to the work of missionaries, and especially that of missionaries in the foreign field.

One of these false conceptions may be denominated the romantic idea of missionary work. Although the whole world is much nearer together to-day than it was forty years ago, and China and Japan are by no means the almost unknown, far-away countries they then were, there is still very much of romance connected with the thought of going to the other side of the world and entering into the midst of oriental scenes and customs; to find one's self surrounded by strange-looking people; to exchange the familiar oak and elm and maple for the giant banyan, the fragrant camphor, and the beautiful palm. There is much that is fascinating about the Orient. The enchantment of the *Arabian Nights* is thrown around the dreamer; he walks amid scenes of indescribable magnificence, and revels in the realm of the weird and the mysterious. There is a sure and certain remedy for all this—namely, actual entrance upon the foreign missionary work; but it is a rather costly remedy for the Church which sends out such a dreamer to its work at the front. The actual contact with heathenism in all its degradation; the observation of the great prevalence of skin diseases, so that one comes heartily to appreciate the native's method of salutation—by joining his own hands and shaking them at you rather than by shaking hands with you; the sad revelation which is soon made that the third plague of Egypt still prevails in the glorious lands of the Orient, and that the industrious insects which delight so much in establishing a joint occupancy of your body abound everywhere; the sight of men covered with loathsome sores exposing themselves to view upon the bridges and in other conspicuous places; the realization that if an oriental country is one in which "the eye is regaled" it is also one in which "the nose is assailed;" the depressing effect of constant contact with superstition and vice—all these, and a hundred other things, speedily dissipate all romantic ideas, and leave the missionary who has gone out to the ends of the earth under the inspiration of romance "a sadder, but a wiser man." It is safe to say that no man ever goes out to a heathen field the second time from any impulse of romance. His first sojourn there cures him effectually of that.

There is another conception of missionary work which may be denominated the experimental idea. That is to say, a young minister, looking about for a field in which to operate, hears of certain openings in the great foreign missionary field. He says to himself, "Well, I do not know whether I should like that kind of work or not. There is a great deal about it that seems to me pleasant. The novelty connected with it and the spice of danger in sea-voyages and residence in an oriental country have a sort of charm for me. I have a notion to go and try it a while. If I do not like it I can come back; and the experience I get will be useful to me." This is no fancy sketch, for there have been missionaries whose course of thinking and decision in regard to entering upon the work is accurately described in the words here used. But this is also an utterly false conception of the spirit with which missionary work should be entered upon. No man entering upon the work with such sentiments as these is qualified for his vocation; nor has the Church any right to expect success in connection with his labors.

Another false conception of missionary work is that which regards it as a means of getting knowledge of foreign countries and foreign things, and

which therefore leads men into it from motives of
curiosity. The acquisition of knowledge is, beyond
question, very desirable, and when pursued under
proper circumstances is in every way commendable,
but Christian missions were not instituted as a
means for the aquisition of secular knowledge by
those who engage in them. A man may have a
special bent for the attainment of knowledge in regard to foreign countries, the character of their inhabitants, their mineral and agricultural resources,
the peculiarity of their languages, and many other
things of this kind. Such knowledge is useful. It
is right for a Christian man to give proper attention
to it. But when one is weighing the question in
his mind, Shall I go as a missionary to the foreign
field?—to decide that question upon the opportunities that will be furnished him to gratify his curiosity in these particulars is treason to the Master
whom he professes to serve. The object to which
he has consecrated his life is not the acquisition of
geographical, botanical, mineralogical, or ethnolog-
ical knowledge, but the salvation of human souls;
the conquest of the world for Christ.

Still another false conception of missionary work
is that which regards it as a means of contributing
to the world's store of philology, archæology, and
kindred sciences. Young men are very apt, during
their years of school and college life, to acquire a
taste for research in some particular branch of
study. Some become intensely interested in the

study of languages; their origin and development, their root words, and the relations of these to those of other languages. Others become very fond of the study of antiquities. Everything ancient has a special charm for them, and it is their joy to explore the hidden treasures of ancient times. Of course the great oriental nations furnish a fine field for study in these particular lines and the problems of language presented for solution awaken a keen mental appetite, while a vast field for antiquarian research also opens before them. No word is uttered against the usefulness of these studies or the propriety of pursuing them. We are simply considering the proper and the false conceptions of missionary work, and must pronounce that an utterly wrong conception which allows a candidate to think of it as a means by which he may contribute to enlighten the world in regard to philology, archæology, or any kindred science. The science to which he as a missionary of Christ is called to give heed is the science of salvation through the sacrifice of Christ made available to all men through faith in him.

Another false conception of missionary work is that which leads one to enter upon it with the idea of helping to civilize and elevate the nations. To a civilized and cultivated man the sight of nations in barbarism, or in a semi-civilized condition, is one of sadness. The humane impulse is at once aroused to contribute to their civilization and to elevate

(3) 33

them from their present low condition. This is a noble and philanthropic desire. It does credit to the head and heart of him who entertains it. It presents a worthy object of pursuit, to which a humane man might well devote the energies of his life. But it is not the work of the Christian missionary, except, it may be, incidentally. His work is of a deeper, more radical, more far-reaching kind. He deals with the very springs of human action; he seeks to secure the regeneration of men's souls; and it is a low and unworthy conception of the work for a missionary of the gospel to look upon it only as a civilizing and elevating agency. A man does not need to be a minister, nor even a Christian, to engage in that work; a civilized man with humane impulses may take it up as a vocation. And, this being the case, it must certainly be a very inadequate conception of missionary work which looks upon it only as a means to such an end.

There are many other misconceptions of the missionary work of the Church, and of the missionaries who go out under her commission, but these will serve as specimens and will sufficiently indicate the principles which should guide us in coming to a right conclusion. Let us briefly summarize them:

It is a false conception of the Church's missionary work to look upon it, 1. As a merely benevolent agency. 2. As merely a civilizing and educating agency. 3. As simply one department of Church work.

False conceptions of the work of the missionary are those which look upon it, 1. As a romantic work. 2. As an experimental work. 3. As an opportunity to gratify curiosity. 4. As a means of contributing to the world's store of knowledge. 5. As a work of civilizing and elevating the nations.

What, then, is the true conception of missionary work?

Simply this: It is the work of the Christian Church for which it was organized, and for the accomplishment of which it exists. What is the Christian Church? Is it not the organized body of Christ's followers? What is it here for? Is it not for this one purpose: to "go into all the world, and preach the gospel to every creature"? Nothing is clearer, from a careful consideration of the constitution of the Church of Christ, than that missionary work is the function of the Church as such. It is not a benevolence, which appeals to the hearts of Christian people and to which they may give more or less attention according to circumstances. It does not bear the outside, though affiliated, relation to the Church that an Orphan Asylum might, or an Institution for the Blind. It is not merely a grand agency among many others for enlightening and civilizing the world. It is not simply a department of Church work. It is the one vital, all-absorbing, specific work of the Church; and all departments of work are valuable and justifiable just in proportion as they bear upon the accomplishment of this work.

The Sunday-school is valuable because it helps in a very efficient way this great work of the Church, to bring the gospel to every creature, by taking that gospel to the minds and the hearts of the young and bringing them to Christ in their early days. Education is valuable because it develops the mental powers, and enables those who obtain it to do better work for God in the use of their trained intellects in his service. The Tract cause is valuable because it takes the truths of the gospel in a very convenient and efficient shape to multitudes of men. And so we may go through all the agencies of the Church and show that the only reason they have for existence as Church agencies at all is that they contribute to this, the one great work of the Church: to give the gospel to every creature; to make disciples of all nations.

The great work of a temperance organization is to save men from drunkenness. If it teaches hygiene it is that men may see the evil effects of alcohol upon the human system. If it seeks for repressive law it is that temptations to drunkenness may be taken away. But no one would think of speaking of the effort to save men from drunkenness as one of the agencies, one of the purposes, of the society. That is *the* purpose of the Society; the sole reason for its existence. The other work which it does is incidental and auxiliary to that. So the work of the Christian Church is to take the gospel to the world; and its Sunday-schools, its tract

agencies, its educational institutions, are all incidental to that, its great work, and are justified as
proper agencies to be used by the Church only as
they contribute to that for which it exists.

We have no right to take missionary work from
the place to which Christ himself assigned it, the
work of his Church in the world, and put it in any
subordinate position. It is not allowable to class
it among the many desirable agencies for helping
on the Redeemer's kingdom, much less to allow
Christ's people to look upon it as among optional
benevolences, to be engaged in or not according to
their view of present necessities and present resources. We need to get it into the minds and into
the hearts of Christians that there is one great purpose for which the Church of Christ was instituted
on earth, and that purpose is the bringing of his gospel to every human heart. Therefore the test by
which every proposition to engage the Church in any
form of activity ought to be decided is, "Will this
help to accomplish the work of taking the gospel to
every creature?"

If our reasoning is correct it follows that the
missionary spirit is an absolute necessity to true
church life. Air is not more necessary to the body
than the missionary spirit is to a church of Christ.
A church which is destitute of that spirit, which has
no ardent longing for the salvation of the world,
which is content with its elegant building and its
comfortably cushioned pews, in which its members

may pleasantly listen to pulpit oratory on the Sabbath, while no duty is felt and no effort put forth for the salvation of the world, is a dead church; a beautiful form, perhaps, but lifeless as a marble statue. What right has any church to expect success—nay, what apology has it for existence, while neglecting the work which its divine Head has assigned to it?

It follows, too, that the very best credential of a church's genuineness is its active missionary labor. When the Master says "Go," the church which most promptly goes shows thereby its greatest fidelity to him. When he commands, "Preach the gospel to every creature," the church which is most active in planning to take the gospel to all who are destitute of it, and in wisely executing those plans, is the church which gives best evidence of its genuine character. When he says "Make disciples of all nations," the church which, refusing to bound its circle of duties and activities by the limits of "the parish," eagerly seeks to do its full share in reaching out after the nations that "sit in darkness, and in the shadow of death"—that is the church which bears the impress of its Lord, and gives to the world the best proof of being in accord with him.

To secure this proper conception of the relation of missionary work to the church we must begin with the individual Christian. We must seek to have every church member realize that "None of us liveth to himself;" that the first duty of a converted soul is to go out after others—a duty not to be discharged by proxy. There are many Christians, blessed with a considerable amount of wealth, who would gladly buy off from duty in this matter by the payment of money to support those who will do it; but they need to do unselfish, sacrificing work for others in order that they may come into vital union with a self-sacrificing Saviour. They need to feel that they are not their own, that they are bought with a price; and that he who has purchased them with his own precious blood has given them a work to do. Active, aggressive individual Christians will make an active, aggressive Christian church. Such a church will not be content to exhaust its efforts within its own limits, but will be continually seeking for opportunities to push the conquests of the gospel into other regions.

An aggregation of such aggressive individual churches in a country will make a great, active, missionary Church whose operations will push out into all the world, taking the blessings of the gospel to the whole needy, perishing race.

It would seem, too, that sanctified Christian wisdom would lead all the great branches of Christ's Church to some concerted and unified action for the accomplishment of the great work. As it would be folly for a dozen regiments to attack a common enemy without any concert of action—all massing in one direction, and leaving much of the enemy's territory without attention; or scattering here and there in feeble bands and without any common plan —so it does not seem wise for the great branches of Christ's army to be carrying on the warfare against his enemy without any reference to each other, without any consistent plan of action, without any comprehensive view of the whole work to be done and the best arrangement of forces for doing it. Given the work to be done—the subjugation of the world to Christ; and the forces to accomplish it—the body of believers throughout the world; it is not too much to say that there ought to be conference between the great branches of the Church as to the occupancy of fields, surveying the whole ground and deciding upon the best way to occupy it and speedily bring the world to Christ.

It would not be a mistranslation of the words of our Saviour in his great intercessory prayer to render them: "As thou hast made me a missionary to the world, so have I made them missionaries to the world." The missionary idea is at the root and foundation of the Christian Church. Its whole spirit and life is missionary. And it must carry on the missionary work as the great function for which it was created. It is therefore not at liberty to delegate this work to an independent society, but it is bound to take it up and prosecute it as the very work for which it was brought into existence; which it has divine authority to prosecute and is under divine obligation to perform.

CHAPTER III

THE CALL AND QUALIFICATIONS OF MIS-
SIONARIES

IF the view of the Great Commission presented in the First Chapter be correct it follows that a call to the ministry is a call to a share in the work instituted by that commission; namely, to "go into all the world and preach the gospel to every creature;" to "make disciples of all the nations." The particular portion of the great field in which any minister shall labor is to be determined by the leadings of the Holy Spirit, by special impressions as to personal duty, and by the call of the proper authorities. There was once a prevalent sentiment which regarded missionaries as quite a separate class in the Christian ministry, who must be distinctly called out from the common ranks and feel themselves impelled to consecrate their lives to the mission work, and who must then be put under special conditions and assume various solemn obligations not imposed upon the ministry in general. The view which has come to be quite generally entertained of later years was expressed by Dr. John M. Reid, the late Honorary Secretary of the Missionary Society of the Methodist Episcopal Church, at the Decennial Missionary Conference at Calcutta, in 1883, when he said: "Once the missionaries were sent out with most minute instructions: now we send them out with only such obligations as any minister has assumed, and we commit the assignments to work and all details of the missions entirely to themselves. It is needless to say we are gratified with the result."

Regarding the call to the ministry as a call to the great work of the Church in evangelizing the world, it is well to spend a few moments in considering it.

This call includes, 1. A firm persuasion on the part of its subject that it is his duty to devote himself to the preaching of the gospel; 2. Providential indications of duty such as are developed in the bent of one's mind, in a strong desire awakened in the heart, in a sense of dissatisfaction or a feeling of being out of place in other pursuits; and 3. The coincident belief of the church that the person is called to the work. The agent in the call is the Holy Spirit. The manner in which the call is communicated varies greatly with different persons. The Holy Spirit is not limited in his methods of operation, but adapts them to the mental and other peculiarities of those upon whom he acts.

Dr. Kidder says: "A comparison of the mental experiences by which a thousand different ministers of any given period have reached the common result of a devout persuasion that they were moved by the Holy Ghost to take upon themselves the sacred office, while it might suggest a classification of experiences, would hardly discover any absolute identity. It would be found that some received distinct impressions of this duty in early childhood, which grew with their growth and strengthened with their strength. Others who received similar impressions sought to reject them, and by a course of sin grieved the Holy Spirit. They put in jeopardy their soul's salvation while endeavoring, Jonah-like, to escape from duty; nevertheless the Spirit strove with them, and before it was wholly too late they yielded to his call. Some had distinct impression of this duty before their conversion, and some even for a long period refused to seek God in their unwillingness to acknowledge his claims upon them to preach the gospel. On some minds the conviction of ministerial duty flashed with the suddenness of a startling revelation. To others it came almost imperceptibly, like the gradual dawning of the day. Still others have received the divine call in the same voice which uttered their pardon. To some it has been made known in silence and solitude, to others in the midst of public assemblies and under the ministration of the preached word. While some have received the sacred call without the intervention of man, to many others it has been brought with the voice or by the agency of Christian friendship. Some have reached their profoundest convictions by a species of religious instinct; others by slow processes of reasoning and by a careful comparison of conflicting claims and impulses. This call, however brought to the soul, ought to be clear and satisfactory."

No man has a right to expect that a miracle will be wrought to assure him of his call to the ministry, nor that the Spirit's call will be demonstrated by evidence of an absolutely compulsory nature. But this much may be confidently declared: that a person genuinely called will find himself somehow awakened to consideration of personal duty in regard to preaching the gospel so as to lead him to serious inquiry concerning it; such inquiry leading to deeper conviction, and finally to a settled purpose in which conscience is satisfied and there is a sweet persuasion of being in the path of duty.

But, it will be asked, is there not a special and definite call to devote one's self to missionary work, or even to enter some particular field? By no means necessarily. The call to the work of the Christian ministry is sufficient; and any man who responds to that call to enter upon the great work of the Church, "Yes, I'll go, provided I may confine my labors within certain limits that I will designate," proves himself thereby unworthy to enter upon the ministry at all. It is enough that the servant of God, having entered the ministry, shall hold himself ready to exercise it wherever God in his providence may direct. The attention of the proper authorities may be drawn to some particular minister as being specially adapted to foreign missionary work, and when their call is presented to him, if he has it in his heart to reply: "I am ready to go where I am most needed and where I can do the best work for God; if those who know me, and know the work, feel persuaded that I am the man who ought to be sent I am as ready to go to China or Japan or India as to any place in the United States" —that man has the true missionary spirit, has a sufficient missionary call, and may go forth with the expectation of God's blessing.

Have we not examples of special calls to the missionary work? Unquestionably we have. Bishop Thoburn is reported as saying that his call to India was as distinct and unmistakable as his call to the ministry. No one can question the power of the Holy Spirit to impress upon the mind and heart of a person his duty to enter the foreign field, or even to enter some particular part of that field, as distinctly as he made known his will to Paul that he should go over into Macedonia. There are many instances in the history of missions of special leadings of the Divine Spirit.

The celebrated Dr. Duff said: "It was when a student at college, in perusing the article on India in Sir David Brewster's Edinburgh Encyclopedia, that my soul was first drawn out as by a spell-like fascination toward India. And when, at a later period, I was led to respond to the call to proceed to India as the first missionary ever sent forth by the established National Church of Scotland, my resolution was, if the Lord so willed it, never, never to return again." Very probably he regarded that "spell-like fascination toward India," though it may not be on record that he ever said so, as the Spirit's call in his heart to labor in that field.

The venerable George Thompson when a young man was thrown into prison in Missouri because of his activity in befriending slaves and helping them to get away where they could be free. From the depths of that Missouri prison he was led to devote himself to the work of God in Africa; a noble resolution to be born in the heart of a young man shut up in a professedly Christian country for helping Africans to freedom—to give his life to taking the gospel to the millions of Africa! There seems to have been in his case a specific call to a particular field. Yet his entry in his diary at the time of his appointment to Africa shows that he was ready for any field. After quoting a number of God's precious promises he writes: "Lord, it is enough; my soul is satisfied. On these promises will I rest. With such assurances I cheerfully leave my father, mother, brothers, sisters, wife and child, house, land, home and country, to go where thou shalt lead. Except thy presence go with me, carry me not up hence. Thy presence going with me, send me any where. 'Here am I; send me.' Only thy will I wish to know. Lead me and guide me to that portion of the field where thou seest I can do most for thee.

'Only thou my Leader be,
And I still will follow thee.'

Any where, any thing, any how, dear Saviour, only glorify thy blessed and lovely name." Ought it not to be the sincere and earnest prayer of every man called into the vineyard of the Lord, "Lead and guide me to that portion of the field where thou seest I can do most for thee"? And if this were the case would there be any lack of supply for any portion of the field?

The biographer of Henry Martyn tells us that one day when he was in company with Mr. Simeon the latter remarked upon the great benefits which had resulted from the services of Dr. Carey, and "Martyn's attention was at once arrested; the vast importance of the missionary cause flashed upon his mind, and his soul was stirred to its depths at the thought of the perishing millions who were without God, without Christ, and without hope in the world." Soon after this, while reading Brainerd's biography, he, filled with a holy emulation, resolved to follow the example of a man who "jeoparded his life unto the death on the high places of the mission field. . . . He was no quixotic enthusiast, no wild adventurer; but he sat down and counted the cost, and was enabled to relinquish much that made life sweet and home dear that he might, like the brave apostle of old, 'preach amongst the Gentiles the unsearchable riches of Christ.' . . . The hour of decision was one of extreme anguish, and at times the struggle amounted to agony. But as he was influenced by the highest motives he chose the thorny path of self-denial rather than the easier one of self-indulgence, and he offered himself as a missionary." In this case the influence of missionary conversation and missionary biography led to mental reasoning and soul-questioning as to duty, which resulted in Martyn's dedication of himself to the missionary work.

I quote yet one more example. Elijah C. Bridgman, when he was about to graduate from Andover Seminary, was called upon on the last day of the term by Mr. David Green, the Assistant Secretary of the American Board, who asked to see him alone, and when they had retired to his room introduced the subject of a mission to China. This was on September 23, 1829. Bridgman says: "In reply I told Mr. Green that the mission was one in which I felt, and long had felt, a deep interest, but had not considered myself as the man for that station; for I had regarded it as one of great interest and responsibility, requiring abilities of the very first order; and, besides, my own mind had been turned more to Southern Europe and Western Asia. I told him, however, that if another man could not be found, and the mission should after due consideration seem to demand such services as mine, he might expect a favorable reply." The next day he writes: "Rose at four o'clock, prayed for divine direction in my future course, and endeavored to submit my ways to God. Shall I go to China? Oh, may the will of the Lord be done!"

Four days later he writes: "As the result of my own views and feeling, I announced my determination to engage in the mission."

Here is the case of one up to the day of his graduation not specially called to the missionary field but consecrated to the service of Christ, ready to go where he is most needed, distrustful of his own abilities but willing to let his brethren judge in regard to his adaptation to the field.

Five days later, with no other call than this, his mind is made up and he goes out to be one of the most faithful, devoted and earnest missionaries the China field has ever known.

No one will have the hardihood to question the missionary character of William Taylor; yet, so far as appears, William Taylor's call to the missionary work is the call he originally received to preach the gospel. His subsequent movements under that call have all been guided by the indications of Providence as they have from time to time appeared to him. Like the founder of Methodism, he regards the world as his parish, and where he is to labor, whether in Maryland, or California, or Australia, or India, or South America, or Africa, is to be decided by circumstances.

From our reasoning on the constitution of the Christian Church and the nature of the Great Commission, and as well from the consideration of the experiences of individual missionaries, we come to the following conclusions:

(4)   49

1. That the call to the work of the Christian ministry is a sufficient call to the missionary work when there are providential indications that one should go to a mission field and the Church through its appointed agencies calls for the service.

2. That in addition to this there may be in some cases a specific and definite call impressed by the divine Spirit upon the heart of a person to enter upon foreign missionary work, or even upon a particular foreign field.

3. The fact that such special calls are sometimes given by no means warrants the conclusion that a person should not enter the work unless he receives such a call. Neither may one excuse himself from mission work by saying that he has no impressions of duty in that direction. Perhaps it is his own fault that he has not. If he has never carefully informed himself as to the claims of the mission field, if he has never conscientiously sought to know his adaptation for it, if he has never earnestly prayed, "Lead me and guide me to that portion of the field where thou seest I can do most for thee," it is not wonderful that he has no impressions of duty; but that is no proof that he ought not to have such impressions, or that he would not have them if he were doing his duty and holding himself in a listening attitude for the voice of God's Spirit.

Having thus considered the missionary's call we next turn our attention to the qualifications demanded of him. Some of them are needed by every minister of the gospel, some of them are peculiar to the calling of a missionary.

1. Sincere piety is an indispensable qualification. Nowhere is a man more out of place than on the mission field who does not thoroughly believe in God, and whose soul does not bow in deepest reverence before him. It is not possible for one to go to preach to the heathen the unsearchable riches of Christ, and to do the work heartily and be sustained in it, unless deep in his own soul is the experience of divine things and constant communion with God.

2. Deep and thorough consecration is a requisite. The character of the service is such that only consecrated hearts can meet its demands. To leave the associations and hallowed friendships of home, to go and dwell among the heathen, to feel that the whole atmosphere around you is unfriendly and fight on with unflagging zeal and a hope that never falters—this is a task too great for an unconsecrated heart. The true missionary is a man who has made a full surrender to his Lord and with his whole heart adopts the words of Charles Wesley:

> " Take my soul and body's powers :
> Take my memory, mind and will;
> All my goods, and all my hours ;
> All I know, and all I feel ;
> All I think, or speak, or do ;
> Take my heart, but make it new.'

3. Common sense is imperatively necessary. No matter how deeply pious a man may be, if he lacks

common sense he is a foreordained failure on the mission field. There is no quality that can take the place of this. Unexpected difficulties, unforeseen emergencies, are constantly arising. The conditions of life are new and complicated. Perplexing questions must be met where counselors of age and experience are not at hand. Under such circumstances there is nothing so helpful and valuable as good, sturdy common sense. If there is a way out it is pretty sure to find it. It is not a panacea for every ill that missionary flesh is heir to, but it comes nearer to being such than anything else. Men of unduly imaginative natures, men like him of whom it was said that he

> "Could plan new planets without the least misgiving,
> But on this planet couldn't make a living,"

are just the sort of men who are not wanted and who are sadly out of place in mission work. Let it be understood that a prime requisite—a *sine qua non*—of missionary qualification is good common sense.

4. A knowledge of human nature is a very desirable qualification. A man may know books without knowing much about men. He may be skilled in reading Latin and Greek but unable to read his nearest neighbor. This is a subtle power, and not easy of accurate definition, yet we all know what it means, and we see that some have it in a marked degree and others are almost destitute of it. Now, on the mission field, this power to know men, to

grasp intuitively the salient points in their characters and thus know how to deal with them, is a
very necessary endowment.

5. Closely allied to this is the power of adaptation. Some men seem never to be able to adjust
themselves to their surroundings; they want the
whole world to be run on the same principle on
which their studies are carried on. But the trouble
is that the world does not run that way. "Many
men of many minds," and of very diverse peculiarities and idiosyncrasies, are to be dealt with. Happy
he who can adapt himself to the people among whom
his lot is cast and to the circumstances by which he
is surrounded. A rigid, unbendable, cast-iron sort
of nature is out of place here. The man required
is one who, like Paul, can become "all things to all
men" in the best sense, and for the best purpose;
namely, that he may "save some."

6. Facility in acquiring language is also a
very desirable qualification. In China, or Japan, or
India, or in almost any foreign field, it is necessary
to learn a new language, and unless the missionary
has some facility in acquiring language he is liable
to be a great bungler in his attempts to speak to the
people. Some of the languages depend largely upon
tones and accents, and upon the nice discrimination
of aspirate and unaspirate initial sounds. It is not
impossible for plodding industry to accomplish
much where this faculty is lacking, but there is a
very great advantage to start with in having a fac-

ulty for language and some love for the study of languages.

7. Most of the missionary societies are disposed to insist that a candidate for service in the foreign field shall have a good wife, devoted to the work. The ancient injunction concerning the bishop or elder, that he should be "the husband of one wife," which the church has generally interpreted as meaning that he should not be the husband of more than one, is applied in a mandatory sense by the societies of to-day to their candidates. Exceptions are occasionally made, but the rule is a good one. It is emphatically not good for man to be alone in a far-off mission field. The comforts of a Christian home are nowhere better appreciated. Then, too, a single man is often looked upon with suspicion where a married man, and the head of a family, is welcomed and trusted. Moreover, the presence of a Christian family, exemplifying the truths of Christian teaching, is always a most healthful and helpful influence in a heathen community, and is the best means of counteracting the unfavorable impressions received from the ungodly conduct of men from Christian countries who live in utter defiance of all the moral precepts of Christianity. Of course, there are some disadvantages also. The wife and mother, with the peculiar burdens incident to her position in an unfriendly climate, is more likely to fail in health than her husband, and it sometimes happens that in the midst of his greatest

usefulness a missionary is obliged to return with his invalid wife. Sometimes, too, the interests of the work demand their separation for a time, and the wife returns home to be recruited in health while the husband remains upon the field. Then, too, arises that most perplexing question, that greatest of missionary trials, when children in the most formative stages of their character must be sent home for education. On account of these things there have not been wanting those who have argued for celibacy among missionaries. But, estimating all the disadvantages at their full worth, it is the almost unanimous opinion of missionaries and of the authorities of missionary societies that it is far better, as a rule, that the missionary should go out as a married man; taking care that his wife has the qualifications that will fit her to share in the glorious work upon which he is about to enter. One word of caution to those preparing for the ministry: Do not go immediately to seeking this particular qualification for missionary service. It will be well to make sure of most of the other qualifications first; and to bring to this matter the mature judgment which the last weeks of the Senior year can supply—or, perhaps better still, make it a post-graduate study.

8. Physical health is a necessary qualification. It is folly to send out to our foreign field a person who is diseased, or one who has marked tendencies to bilious complaints, or one who has inherited weak

lungs. The American Board asks of its candidates: "What is the state of your health? Did you inherit a good constitution in all respects? Are you aware of being now, or of having been at any time, subject to any bodily ailment or infirmity? Are your habits sedentary, or active?" And all the other societies are equally careful in endeavoring to secure healthy, vigorous men as missionaries. It is partly owing to this fact, as well as to their careful habits of living, that the missionaries are by far the healthiest of all foreign residents in the East. Of all the male missionaries connected with the . Foochow Mission of the Methodist Episcopal Church at the end of its first fifty years, only six had died, and only two of those died upon the field.

9. It is requisite that the missionary should possess well cultivated mental powers. It is a great mistake to suppose that his work is among people of a low order of intellect. In the bazars of India, in the wayside audiences of China, in the halls of Japan, he is apt to encounter men accustomed to deep philosophical thought—foemen worthy of his steel. Workmen who are thoroughly prepared, who will have no occasion to be ashamed when brought face to face with the thinkers of the Orient, are urgently demanded for this work.

Other qualifications there are, but these are among the most important.

In deciding upon life work the minister of Christ

should let the claims of the foreign field have a calm, deliberate, honest consideration, and his decision should be such as to meet the approval of his conscience and of God. The spirit of consecration required for it will prove to be the best possible qualification for work at home, should God in his providence order the field to be at home rather than abroad.

CHAPTER IV

HOME ORGANIZATION AND METHODS

IT being the duty of the Church to take the gospel to the whole world sanctified common sense would seem to teach:

1. That we have no right to expect the heathen to be ready to support the gospel as soon as it is presented to them.

2. That we have no right to demand that those who are sent to make known the gospel to the heathen shall support themselves by some manual or other labor.

3. That whatever is needed for their proper support should be supplied by the Church at home. The whole Church being under the obligation, it is manifest that the particular persons who are called out as the executives of the Church in this work must be sustained by the disciples at home.

As it is necessary to raise money to carry on the work let us inquire whether there is any Scriptural rule in regard to this matter. Do we not find the very best rule formulated by the Apostle Paul in 1 Cor. xvi, 2: "Upon the first day of the week let every one of you lay by him in store, as God hath prospered him"?

On this Dr. Wm. Speer has well said: "The most consummate financier in modern ages can add nothing to, and take nothing from, this brief rule. It contains every important principle necessary to the accomplishment of the great end in view. All that is needed is simple obedience to it in order to fill the treasuries of the Christian Church, to secure for the Church that favor of God which follows from conformity to his will, and to supply means sufficient to send the gospel to every creature. It is suited to be a complete, abiding and universal rule. It is one which should be put upon the walls of every house of worship; which should be written in the memory and heart of every professor of religion; and which should be taught to every child that has been consecrated to God in Christian baptism."

Let it be admitted that this rule was given to the church at Corinth, as it had been to the churches in Galatia, with especial reference to securing aid for the suffering Christians at Jerusalem; nevertheless its appropriateness as a rule for Christian giving in general is evident.

It presents giving as a universal duty. "Let every one of you lay by him in store." The poor are not to be excused because they have but little money. That is a good reason why they should give but little, as compared with the rich, but it is no reason why they should not give at all. It is a great deal better for a church to have a hundred dollars given by a hundred poor members than it is to have a hundred dollars given by one rich member. The most successful churches financially are those which come the nearest to securing the giving of something by every member of the church.

This rule contemplates regularity and system in giving: "Upon the first day of the week." Men say, "What is everybody's business is nobody's business," and it may be said, "What is to be done at just any time is done at no time." There is a great advantage in having a regular time set apart for this duty, moreover; it is very much easier to give in this way. Few men would feel it a hardship to give ten cents a week to the Lord's cause, but many of them would be startled at a demand for five dollars at any one time during the year.

This rule also contemplates giving as an act of worship. The regularity would be secured if the second or fifth day of the week were mentioned instead of the first, but the command to do it on the first day connects it with the service of public worship; and there can be no doubt that the glad offering of our substance ought to be considered as much an act of worship as is prayer or praise.

This rule prescribes that giving shall be in proportion to ability or income: "as God hath prospered him." The rich are to give largely, the poor less, but all are to give; to give regularly, and to give according to their means. If this simple rule were carried out it is not difficult to see that the treasury of the church would be amply supplied for all its needs.

The apostle adds, as an effect that would follow the adoption of this rule, "that there be no gatherings when I come." This would shut off giving from mere impulse. The Scripture rule is not impulsive or compulsory giving, but conscientious, regular, proportionate giving. It is one of the most important duties of the ministry to urge upon the people conformity to the Scriptural rule in this matter; and by precept, example and influence to bring the church up to the Bible standard of duty.

One of the best methods for securing money is that prescribed by the Methodist Episcopal Church: "It shall be the duty of the Pastor, aided by the Committee on Missions, to appoint Missionary Collectors, and furnish them with suitable books and instructions, that they may call on each member of the Society, or Church and Congregation, and on other persons, at their discretion, for his or her annual, semi-annual, quarterly, monthly, or weekly contribution for the support of Missions. Said Collectors shall make monthly returns, unless otherwise instructed by the Committee, to the Pastor, or to the Missionary Treasurer of the Church, if there be such Treasurer appointed by the Committee on Missions. Such returns shall be entered in a book, which the Committee shall provide, together with collections and contributions received from other sources. Such entries shall set forth the name of each Collector, the real or assumed names of the contributors, and the amount contributed by each."

This is Scriptural. It contemplates that every member of the church and congregation shall contribute, and shall do it regularly. If it were in thorough operation throughout that Church there would be no difficulty in raising two millions of dollars for missions annually. It is a method which might well be adopted by other denominations.

Another excellent method is the organization of the Sunday-schools as missionary societies. Not only does the steady contribution of small sums by the children and youth of the Sunday-schools greatly increase the aggregate offering of the church, but the missionary exercises held in the Sunday-schools interest the young people of the church in the great work and tend to make the future leaders hearty supporters of the missionary cause.

The monthly missionary prayer meeting ought to be observed in all the churches, and to be made the means of conveying fresh information from the field and calling out the hearty prayers of the members in view of the special needs brought to their notice.

In some of the Churches the administration of the foreign missionary work has been committed to societies organized independently; but it has been seen in most cases that a work which properly belongs to the Church, as such, can only be efficiently carried on by the Church. So it has come to be the case that most of the great Protestant Churches have incorporated the management of their missionary work into the Church itself: intrusting its administration to boards, composed of ministers and laymen, duly elected through the regular channels of their respective ecclesiastical organisms.

Of course these organizations must have capable and efficient executive officers. These are, with hardly any exceptions, the Corresponding Secretaries of the missionary boards. To them is intrusted the correspondence with the various fields, and all the delicate duties of the administration of the affairs of the boards in their relation to the missions and to the individual missionaries. Their office, therefore, is one of the highest trust and responsibility. In addition to this important duty they are also charged with the representation of the work to the ecclesiastical bodies of their respective denominations and to the churches in general. There are no officers in the Church of Christ charged with graver responsibilities, and none whose opportunities for far-reaching service of the most useful and enduring character are greater, than those of the Corresponding Secretaries. They should be upheld by the earnest prayers and the most hearty and sympathetic co-operation of the ministry and laity in all the churches. All that is here said applies also to the godly, efficient and self-sacrificing women who are the Corresponding Secretaries of the various branches of the Women's Foreign Missionary Societies.

CHAPTER V

METHODS AND ADMINISTRATION IN THE FOREIGN FIELD

WHEN a missionary enters any field in which another language than his own is spoken the first work before him is to acquire the language of the people. Something in the way of preaching may be done through an interpreter, but where a mission is established, and there are missionaries and native preachers acquainted with the language, it is not necessary for a new missionary to preach immediately and he is left at liberty to prosecute his study of the language. The time will vary, with the comparative difficulty of the languages and the differing abilities of the men, from a few months in the Spanish-speaking countries to eighteen months or two years in China before one will be fully prepared to preach, though he may converse on ordinary topics considerably sooner.

There are various branches of work in which a missionary may profitably engage, but the main work abroad, as at home, is to preach. The laconic statement of the Methodist Discipline, "The duty of a preacher is: 1. to preach," applies to the whole field, but the circumstances under which he preaches in the foreign field of course differ widely from

64

those of the home field. In many countries he must do much out-door preaching, gathering his audiences in the bazars, in open courts, in the areas of heathen temples, along the waysides, on the sea-shore—where oftentimes, like his Master, he may enter a boat and, making its deck his pulpit, address the people. Frequently he may have occasion to resort to the groves—"God's first temples." Of course his style of address must be adapted to his surroundings. His method must be largely conversational. He must not only allow the people to ask him questions, and that upon a range of subjects which could hardly be allowed in our churches, but he must catechise them with the purpose of finding out the extent of their knowledge in spiritual matters and judging of the kind of instruction best adapted to them. He may sometimes prepare the way for his discourse, as his Master did with the woman of Samaria, by asking for a drink of water. The fact that he is not above asking a favor and the fact that his auditor has done him a service will have much to do with establishing a kindly feeling to begin with. He will do well, too, to follow the Master's example in making his preaching simple, clear and earnest; leading the thoughts of his hearers to the spiritual nature of the one true God and the spiritual character of his worship, and then to the necessity of a mediator to lead us to him. Then, although he may not say, as Christ did, "I that speak unto thee am he," he may say as Ling Ching

Ting, the Chinese preacher, so often did: "Jesus Christ can save you from all your sins; I know it, for he has saved me from mine." This preaching from personal experience is everywhere the very best kind of preaching.

While speaking of the nature of God, in heathen lands, the way is of course open to show the folly of idolatry; then to present proofs of revelation and to tell the ever wondrous story of the cross. It is true that this may be "a stone of stumbling, and a rock of offense" to many, and their feeling may be like that of Hü Yong Mi on his first sight of the New Testament. He says: "Turning over leaf after leaf one name alone was conspicuous on every page and nothing else could I see, the name of Ya-su, Ya-su (Jesus, Jesus). I was disappointed, angry, and in a sudden passion of rage I tore the book to pieces, threw the fragments on the floor, and not satisfied with destroying the book I wished for some sharp implement by which I might expunge the name Ya-su which stared at me from the mutilated pages."

But, although the heathen may rage at the name of Jesus when first presented, they may afterwards be won to it. Hear again from Hü Yong Mi: "Later, on my coming to a knowledge of the doctrine of Christ, I recognized that in this action had been fulfilled the words of the Psalmist, 'They hated me without a cause.' I also thought, with such a disposition the crowd about the cross had cried out, 'Crucify him! Crucify him!' Was I not, indeed, in the same category with them? Alas! A sinner, I knew not that he who in the beginning created man, heaven, earth, and all things, who dwells with the Supreme God, who is the way of eternal life, this One, become Man, was this same Jesus. He who, alone for our sake, descended from heaven, sacrificed his body and shed his blood to redeem us from sin and save us from everlasting death, who commissioned us to attain everlasting life, in endless joy to roam the heavenly plains, was this Jesus. He who corresponded exactly to that for which I had so imploringly longed, so hungered and thirsted, whose salvation I had craved, was Jesus. Him, the source of my life, my ladder of ascent to heaven, my light of true righteousness—why knew I not to love and reverence him, to draw near to him, instead of in anger to pierce and reject him?"

Besides the outdoor preaching there are churches and chapels in which the people can be kept under better control but where the preaching to heathen audiences must be essentially the same. There is this great advantage, however, that in them there is much better opportunity for after meetings, in which direct personal work can often be done to good effect. The Rev. Griffith John gave a good illustration of this. In the General Conference at Shanghai, in 1877, he said: "At the close of one of my services a man followed me into the vestry and addressed me thus: 'I have just heard you say that Christ can save a man from his sins. Can he save me?' 'What sins have you?' I asked. 'Every sin you can think of,' was his reply. Then, reckoning his sins on the tips of his fingers, he said, 'I am an opium smoker, fornicator, gambler, and everything that is bad. Can Christ save me?' I said, 'Yes, Christ can save you.' 'When?' he asked again. 'Now,' was the emphatic reply, 'if you will but trust him for this salvation.' We both prayed, he leading and I following. He was converted then and there, I believe, and at once became one of the most earnest Christians I have ever known. Though not employed as a native agent he is ever making known the way of salvation to his acquaintances. His gospel is Christ the Saviour from sin; and the evidence of Christ's power to save, adduced by him, is the fact that he himself has been thus delivered from the dominion of his own sins by simple faith in the Redeemer. Several have been brought into the church through the instrumentality of this man."

Besides the services for heathen congregations it is often best to hold, especially on the Sabbath, special services for Christians, where the preaching may be more systematic and instruction can be given adapted to the needs of a Christian congregation.

As soon as a few converts are gathered they are organized into a church. The native converts should be instructed from the beginning, however poor they may be, to contribute as they are able for their own church expenses. Very soon some among the converts will show a disposition to preach, and manifest a gift for preaching. Then they can be licensed and sent out. Congregations are gathered by them very frequently in the houses of those who first believe, and then chapels are built; in many places simple and inexpensive, but adequate to the needs of the people. A number of churches gathered in a particular region will soon need organization into a Conference, or Presbytery, or Association, and thus, gradually and naturally, higher ecclesiastical bodies will be formed.

Besides the direct preaching, which is always and everywhere the chief work of the ministry, there are several very important auxiliary agencies. Prominent among these are schools; day schools, in which, along with the ordinary branches of learning, the truths of the gospel can be taught, hold a very important place in mission work. Through these the gospel is brought to the minds of the children and often taken by them to their heathen homes. Boarding schools, academies and colleges will all be demanded as the work advances, and theological seminaries for the training of young preachers are of the highest importance. In addition, considerable help may be given to the native preachers by the missionaries in their periodical visits to the various stations.

The medical work is also an important arm of missionary service. In heathen lands medical knowledge is very crude and imperfect, and surgery almost entirely unknown. It is well to follow in the footsteps of the Master and administer healing to the body as well as to the soul. It is a good way to get to the hearts of the people, and to open many doors to the entrance of the gospel which might otherwise remain closed.

Woman's work, as carried on by the women's missionary societies of the different churches, is one of the most effective agencies of the work. The seclusion in which women of the higher classes in China and India are kept renders this special work of consecrated Christian women for their heathen sisters one of special importance. Their teaching in schools, their instruction and supervision of Bible women, their wonderful work in medicine and surgery, all are telling with immense power in heathen lands.

The distribution of Christian literature is another vast agency for good. Bibles and tracts, hymn books, Christian biographies, and school-books, are printed wherever Christian missions are found. Closely connected with this is the work of translation. A Christian literature is to be provided for the growing Christian communities; the Bible is to be translated into the general languages and the local dialects, older and imperfect translations to be revised, books of every useful kind to be translated or composed.

It will readily be seen that the mission field affords opportunity for the exercise of every variety of talent and gives abundant scope for all peculiarities of mental disposition. With its evangelistic, its educational and its linguistic demands, and its intellectual combats with able thinkers, all classes of consecrated talent will find full employment. In all this work it must constantly be kept in mind that the object to be accomplished is to bring the gospel, with all its blessings, to every creature. Schools, medical work and all other agencies are subordinate and auxiliary to the preaching of the gospel, and are to be cherished in proportion to their efficiency in aiding to bring about the grand result of discipling the nations. It must be noted, too, that the best and most useful men in our foreign fields have been brought in through the preaching of the gospel and have been trained in the work. On the other hand, it must be remembered that these very men are most earnest for the establishment of schools and for a thorough training of young men for the work.

It is important, moreover, to keep constantly in mind that the good to be attained is the establishment of a self-supporting, self-governing and self-propagating church. Anything which tends to pauperize the native church, and lead it to lean perpetually on the home church, is to be carefully avoided; tendencies to keep the reins of government in the hands of the foreign missionary are to be guarded against; the idea must be early implanted in the minds of native Christians that they must propagate the gospel in their own land and in neighboring regions.

It is evident that the evangelization of all the great heathen countries must be accomplished by natives. As Bishop Thomson said to the Chinese Christians, "We have brought the cross to your shores; you must take it up and carry it through the Empire." As the Rev. R. S. Hardy, of India, said at the Liverpool Conference: "The truth must be naturalized; it must cease to be regarded as an exotic before it can thoroughly permeate and permanently regenerate any given nation."

All will agree that China must be evangelized by Chinese, Japan by Japanese, and every great country by its own natives; but as soon as the question of employing native agency comes up we find two antagonistic opinions developing. The matter is necessarily very intimately connected with the self-support of the native churches; and while all agree that the native church should become self-supporting as rapidly as possible, and that the salaries of native preachers should not be beyond the ability of the native churches when fully established, or such as to remove them in style of living from the people, there is great difference of opinion on this one point: should any native preacher be employed by, and paid with the money of, the foreign missionary society? There are some who hold that no native should be employed as a preacher, and certainly never ordained, until he is wholly supported by the native church. Such arguments as these are used:

1. The voluntary labors of a man in hours outside of his daily work are more valuable than his whole time when he is paid for it.

2. Paying native preachers presents a temptation to go into the work for money.

3. The payment of wages to native preachers tends to dwarf, if not to extinguish, voluntary service.

4. It retards self-support.

5. It makes the missionaries sole judges of the qualifications of preachers, to receive and dismiss them at pleasure, which is ecclesiastically wrong.

In answer to this it is said:

1. If voluntary labors are more valuable than paid labor it must be so everywhere; and the argument, if it proves anything, proves too much, and is destructive of the ministry as a body set apart to a special work.

2. The payment of wages will be no temptation to enter the work for money if the amount paid is not more than the person could earn in another employment; especially when he is subject to persecutions and trials as a preacher from which he would otherwise be free.

3. The payment of wages to men who give their whole time to the work ought not to hinder voluntary service on the part of those who have remunerative employment.

4. It ought not to retard self-support if only a moderate sum is paid, and if the native church is instructed from the outset that it must do its utmost to support its own ministry.

5. In the beginning of missions it is a matter of necessity that the missionaries should exercise much power in the selection, employment and dismissal of native agents. But as soon as churches can be organized the members can be trained to their appropriate share in the matter.

Many missionaries feel that, when among the converts we find men of piety, zeal, self-sacrificing spirit, understanding the word of God and having a personal experience of divine things, glad to go and preach the gospel, it would be wrong to wait until a native church should grow up, able to support them, before they should be sent forth to use their powers for the furtherance of Christ's kingdom.

Dr. Blodget voiced the sentiment of this class when he said at the Shanghai Conference: "The churches in China may educate at their own expense young men from Mongolia or Korea and support them afterward while preaching the glad tidings to their own countrymen. Why may not the churches in the United States or England in like manner educate and support Chinese preachers? The Chinese Christians are poor. There are among them those who are desirous of preaching the gospel. Is there anything in the word of God, or in the example of Christ, to hinder our affording such aid to them as they may require?"

The author may repeat what he said at the same Conference:

"The path of truth and safety in this, as in most other matters, lies probably between the two extremes. With so large a field before us, and some converted men ready and qualified to preach the gospel, it certainly does not seem to be the wisest policy to wait for a church to grow up and become able to support them before they are sent forth. Why may we not as well employ a missionary from Foochow at Yenping, as one from America at Foochow? The fact that we can employ ten of the former with the same amount of money that is required for one of the latter certainly constitutes in itself no objection to their appointment; nor can it be shown that it is better to leave all such outlying regions to occasional visits from the missionary, or to draw on the home Church for men and means to occupy them permanently, than to send out native preachers for the time being at the expense of western churches.

"The proper conclusion, then, seems to be: Employ suitable men to preach the gospel to their heathen countrymen; but as soon as members are received into church fellowship accustom them, from the very first, to give according to their ability for the support of the gospel. And, that they may do this the more speedily, carefully avoid placing the

salary of the native preacher at too high a figure—
such as the native church will be unable to pay, and
from which the native preacher will be unwilling to
come down. This is not a case to which 'facilis est
descensus' will apply."

As indicating the feeling which is sometimes en-
gendered among native preachers, and some of the
dangers to be guarded against, take the following
from the remarks of Ram Chandra Bose at the
Decennial Conference in India:

"The salary question is an important factor, and
should not be thrown into the background. The
men raised have a right to be paid. If doctors, law-
yers and undertakers, who are said to feed upon
human misfortunes, have a right to be paid, *they*
certainly have. By whom are they to be paid? By
those who, under God, send them forth. John Wesley's mother is said often to have sent her children
to bed with a blessing but without a supper. If the
Queen of England were to adopt this course her
conduct would justly be censured, that being absolutely wrong in her which was right in poor Mrs.
Wesley. In the same way the course adopted by
the poor church at Jerusalem, in the matter of sending out preachers in the days of the apostles, would
be wrong if adopted by the rich churches of Christendom to-day. These can make a provision for the
preachers they send, and are therefore bound to see
that they are provided for. These are the churches
that appoint native preachers through the instru-

mentality of their agents here, and they are equally bound to see that these preachers are provided for. Nothing can be plainer than this. But it has been said that the paying system has demoralized the native preachers. Not more certainly than it has the missionaries! If the non-paying system is the right system it ought to be adopted in the case of the missionary as well as in that of his assistants."

Native preachers thus employed ought to have as good a theological training as possible, but it is not always best that it should be in a theological school. Rev. R. B. Lyth, of the Fiji Mission, with fourteen hundred church members, found it best to train the native preachers *in* the work, *for* the work. He found they could not endure the close confinement of an institution, but with plenty of work and exercise they would come to their studies with zest. Dr. Mason, of the Toungoo Mission in Burmah, found it best to take his students out with him, as he walked toward the groves at the approach of evening, asking them questions and instructing them along the way. The early Serampore missionaries gave most of their instruction to helpers while they were engaged in the work. This also was largely the case in all the missions in China. Where theological schools are established it is quite customary to send the students out in the surrounding regions to preach.

In selecting native preachers careful inquiry must be made as to their possession of "gifts, grace and usefulness." The evidence in regard to this must first be weighed by the missionaries. When there is a native church the judgment ought to be the joint judgment of the church and the missionaries until the native church is self-supporting, when it may and ought to be allowed to be also self-governing.

As mission work advances, what ought to be the rule in regard to making changes in the habits and customs of the people?

Clearly, we ought to require that all habits and customs which are superstitious, indecent or unchristian shall be abolished; with innocent customs there should be no interference. It is no part of our business to dictate what kind of clothes a people shall wear, but in those regions where it is not the custom to wear clothes at all it is right to insist on a change. The Chinaman's cue being a badge of his loyalty to the present government, and the wearing of the hair in that way being no sin, we have no right to ask him to abandon it. The cramping of the feet of girls being cruel, and therefore unchristian, must be given up. The custom of allowing every one who pleases to come to the house of a newly married couple on the evening of their wedding, and to tease and blackguard the bride as they please, being inhumane and unchristian, must be abolished. The rule given will generally be found easy of application.

As to the administration of missions, it is generally conducted in accordance with the principles of the denomination to which the missionaries belong; although the most strenuous Congregationalist will often find it necessary to exercise pretty ample episcopal powers in the initial stages of mission work, and some will retain them, either through the force of habit or a natural fondness for domination, after the necessity for it has passed away.

In Methodist Episcopal Missions the bishop in charge has the same authority as in a home Conference. When he is present at the annual session he fixes the appointments. During the year he may of course make any changes he deems advisable. The Discipline provides that

"When a Mission is established in a foreign country, or in the United States and Territories outside of Annual Conferences, the Bishop having Episcopal Supervision of the same shall appoint a Member of the Mission as Superintendent, who may also be the Presiding Elder of a District. It shall be the duty of the Superintendent, in the absence of a Bishop, to preside at the Annual Meeting of the Mission, to arrange the work, and take general supervision of the entire Mission, and to represent the state of the Mission and its needs to the Bishop having charge, and to the Corresponding Secretaries."

The Annual Meeting referred to is composed of all the missionaries and native preachers, and has, "in all ecclesiastical matters, the functions and privileges of a District Conference." It also transacts "such other business as may be assigned by the Board, or grow out of the local interests of the work."

It is customary, in missions in which the members are not too widely scattered, to have monthly or quarterly meetings to act upon all questions that may arise in the prosecution of the work, decisions being made by a majority vote.

The mental peculiarities and the innocent habits and usages of the people should have careful consideration in the framing of ecclesiastical organizations. The general harmony prevailing among missionaries of different denominations and their willingness to learn from each other, to "prove all things," and to "hold, fast that which is good," are reasons for hopefulness in regard to the church of the future in the great mission fields.

CHAPTER VI

ORIGIN AND GROWTH OF PROTESTANT FOREIGN MISSIONS

WITHOUT doubt the seeds of foreign missions were sown in the Reformation, and we have some indications of the fact here and there: as, for instance, the wish expressed by Erasmus that the Gospels and Epistles "were translated into all languages, so that they might be read and understood, not only by Scots and Irishmen, but also by Turks and Saracens;" and the expression of his belief that in Asia and Africa "there are surely barbarous and simple tribes who could be easily attracted to Christ if we sent men among them to sow the good seed."

In 1555 Admiral Coligny, afterward leader of the Huguenots, who was among the martyrs of the St. Bartholomew massacre, sent fourteen missionaries to Brazil, two of whom had been chosen by Calvin; but the Portuguese soon put an end to this Protestant colony.

Gustavus Vasa, of Sweden, sent a mission to the Lapps in 1559, opened schools among them, and had Swedish books translated into their language.

The Dutch did some missionary work as they advanced into the Orient, driving the Portuguese

(6) 81

out of Malaysia and Southern India. The work of Grotius on the *Evidences of Christianity* was written as a text book for Dutch missionaries in their preaching to the heathen; and it is said that he personally interested seven jurists of Lubeck to go out to the East as missionaries. Peter Heiling went to Abyssinia in 1632. As early as 1612, Walaeus, a Professor in the University of Leyden, instituted a college for training missionaries. In 1637 eight missionaries were sent out to the Dutch West Indies on the request of the Governor General at Pernambuco.

The followers of John Huss in Bohemia formed themselves into "the Church of the Brethren of the Love of Christ" in 1457, and ten years later, uniting with some of the Waldenses and the Moravians notwithstanding many severe persecutions, they became the *Unitas Fratrum,* better known as the Moravian Church. This martyr church was nearly exterminated by the Jesuit "Anti-Reformation" under Ferdinand II, in 1617; nevertheless, there was a remnant of faithful ones through the century and in 1722 some of them emigrated to an estate of Count Zinzendorf, in Saxony; where, on June 17, 1722, the first tree was felled for the settlement of Herrnhut, since so widely known as the headquarters of the Moravian Church and of its great missionary activities. It is said of Count Zinzendorf that at four years of age he made this covenant with Christ: "Be thou mine, dear Saviour, and I will be thine." At the age of ten he became a pupil of Franke, at Halle, where he formed circles for prayer and organized his fellow students as "The Order of the Grain of Mustard Seed," which pledged them to seek the conversion of others—of heathen and Jews. He married Erdmuth Dorothea, a lady of rank; but they cast all rank aside and covenanted to be ready to go to the heathen, staff in hand. They were glad to find the Moravian refugees at the Count's estate of Berthelsdorf. The Count consecrated his property to the work of forming circles of pious people within the Lutheran Church. When Dober and Nitschmann set out for St. Thomas, West Indies, in 1732, they were willing to become slaves themselves in order to reach the slaves to whom they went. In 1733 the Moravians began their work in Greenland which has met with such marked success, in 1734 their work among the Indians in New York and Pennsylvania, and in 1735 a missionary was sent to the Indians in South America. In later years they have taken up work in Africa, Australia, India and Tibet; and their missions have grown until they have 100,000 persons in their congregations.

George Fox, the Leicestershire shoemaker who founded the Society of Friends, wrote, about 1643: "All Friends everywhere, that have Indians or blacks, you are to preach the gospel to them and other servants, if you be true Christians; for the gospel of salvation was to be preached to every

creature under heaven." In 1661 three of his followers were moved to go towards China and
Prester John's country. Of these, Richard Costrop
fell ill and died, while John Stubbs and Henry Fell
reached Alexandria and there delivered their mes-.
sage to Turk, Greek, and Papist. George Robinson obeyed "a call" to preach in Jerusalem. Mary
Fisher faced the sultan Mahomet IV with impunity.

The Pilgrims who sailed in the Mayflower in
1620 were missionaries. Though Robinson wrote
to the Governor of New Plymouth, "Oh that you
had converted some before you had killed any!"
yet one of their number was set apart to labor for
the conversion of the Indians. In the charter which
Charles I gave to the colony of Massachusetts it
was asserted that "the principal end of the planta-
tion was to win and invite the natives of the country
to the knowledge of the only true God and Saviour
of mankind, and the Christian faith;" in 1646 the
Colonial Legislature accordingly passed an act for
the propagation of the gospel among the Indians.

The first missionary society among Protestants
was created by an act of the Long Parliament,
under Cromwell, in 1649, which chartered the
"Corporation for the Propagation of the Gospel in
New England." Eliot and the Mayhews were
helped by this Society, and "Mistress Bland," the
first English woman missionary. John Eliot, born
in 1604, reached Boston in 1630, was ordained
Presbyterian minister of Roxbury, and gave the

last fifty-eight years of his life, ending in 1690, to
the evangelizing of the Pequot tribe of the Iro-
quois Nation. He formed the first church of
Red Indians at Natick in 1660, and printed the Mo-
heecan Bible, at Cambridge, 1661-3. Before his
death there were eleven hundred members in six
Indian churches. The Moheecans became extinct
in the subsequent wars, and in 1836 one hut, with
four half-breed inmates, represented all that was
left of his work.

The East India Company, chartered first in 1600,
could not claim in any other than an unconscious
and unintentional manner to have been a missionary
agency. Chaplain Terry, of Sir Thomas Roe's
embassy, sent by James I to the Great Mogul, reported that the natives said of the English, "Christian religion devil religion; Christians much drunk;
Christians much do wrong; much beat; much
abuse others." This has unfortunately continued
to be true of very many for two and a half centuries.
Nevertheless the charter of the United East India
Company, given in 1708 by King William III, con-
tained provisions for a missionary establishment.
The ministers were to learn the language of the
people, "the better to enable them to instruct the
Gentoos in the Protestant religion." But the first
missionaries sent avowedly to evangelize the natives of India were sent by the Danish Government
and the German Pietists—namely, Ziegenbalg and
Plütschau—and their work was almost entirely con-

fined to the territory in Tranquebar that was under Danish rule.

Christian Friedrich Schwartz, of Sonnenberg, Prussia, born in 1726, died in 1798, was granted a free passage to India with his company, by the East India Company, in 1750. His labors in Tanjore, Tinnevelly and elsewhere met with much success, and he must be considered the founder of the native church in Southern India, which now numbers five hundred thousand people. He is worthy of perpetual remembrance among the early founders of Protestant missions.

The first Protestant missionary to Calcutta was a Swede, Kiernander, of the Danish-Halle Mission at Cuddalore, who went to Calcutta in 1758 on the invitation of Lord Clive himself. At the end of twenty-eight years of missionary work he had two hundred and nine heathens and three hundred Romanists as converts. Mr. Charles Grant, who at first went out to Bengal as a trader, was instrumental in opening missionary work in North India. He and those associated with him sent home for eight missionaries, of whom Grant was to support two. The men were sent out, and spent three years at Benares in the study of the native languages, but their hopes were not realized owing to the opposition of the East India Company.

The idea of a world-wide propagation of the gospel does not seem to have taken any hold upon Protestant Christians in England until the Eighteenth Century had made much progress. Rev. Robert Millar, a Presbyterian minister in Paisley, published in 1723 his *History of the Propagation of Christianity and the Overthrow of Paganism,* in which he urged effort for the conversion of the heathen world. In 1744, after some remarkable revivals of religion had occurred, a number of ministers who felt awakened to duty in this regard established "a concert to promote more abundant application to a duty that is perpetually binding— prayer that our God's kingdom may come, joined with praises." This was to be observed on Saturday evening and Sunday morning, with a special solemn observance on the first Tuesday of each quarter. This had a rapid spread in England, and in 1746 a memorial was sent to Boston inviting all Christians in America to pledge themselves to join in it for the next seven years. Out of this grew the celebrated work of Jonathan Edwards, *"A Humble Attempt to Promote Explicit Agreement and Visible Union of God's People in Extraordinary Prayer for the Revival of Religion."* This work came into the hands of William Carey, and had great influence on his mind. This season of awakening also gave birth to the first missionary hymns. Watts's grand hymn paraphrasing the 72d Psalm, "Jesus shall reign where'er the sun," was written in 1719, Williams's "O'er the glowing hills" in 1722, and Shrubsole's "Arm of the Lord" about the same time.

CHAPTER VII

FORMATION OF BRITISH MISSIONARY SOCIETIES

BAPTIST MISSIONARY SOCIETY

IT was in 1784 that action was taken which may fairly be considered as inaugurating the modern era of Protestant Missions. This was at Nottingham, at a meeting of the Associate Baptist Churches, when John Sutcliff, minister of Olney, moved to arrange for meetings to "earnestly implore a revival of our churches and of the general cause of our Redeemer." In the plan, which was drawn up by John Ryland, Jr., of Northampton, other Christian societies were cordially invited to join, and "the spread of the gospel to the most distant parts of the habitable globe" was named as "the object of your most fervent requests."

In 1780 William Carey (born in Paulerspury, Eng., Aug. 17, 1761) was baptized by Ryland in the river Nen. In 1781 this journeyman shoemaker united with eight others to form the Baptist church in the hamlet of Hackleton. There he preached his first sermon, and in 1787 he was ordained by Andrew Fuller to the ministry at Moulton village. He was constantly pondering on the state of the heathen, and longing to go as a missionary to Otaheite.

In 1792 the Baptist Missionary Society was formed at Kettering and Carey was its first missionary. At the meeting on October 2 Carey had preached from Isaiah liv, 2, 3, laying down his two great mottoes, "Expect great things from God," "Attempt great things for God." Retiring to the little parlor of the widow Beeby Wallis, twelve ministers subscribed £13, 2s. 6d. and organized what they then named "The Particular Baptist Society for Propagating the Gospel among the Heathen." November 10 of the next year, 1793, Carey, with Mr. Thomas, formerly a surgeon on an East Indian ship, landed at Calcutta, notwithstanding the opposition of the East India Company. India had by that time become, under Lord Cornwallis, virtually a Christian empire. Carey undertook to live on the self-support system of the Moravian brotherhood, but in tropical India the attempt to preach and support himself and family by his own labor was disastrous, and they were in danger of starvation. He then engaged in the manufacture of indigo at Dinajpore, and spent five years in perfecting his knowledge of Bengalee—of which he wrote a grammar and into which he translated the New Testament —learned Sanskrit, established a printing press, and planned new missions, all at his own cost. His first converts were chiefly European officials, and he formed a church. Four colleagues arrived in 1799, of whom Marshman and Ward became imperishably associated with Carey as the pioneer missionaries of India. They were established at **Serampore**, on the north bank of the Hoogly, fourteen miles above Calcutta. This became the fountain of life and light for all Southern Asia. The three families lived at the same table, at a cost of a little over five hundred dollars a year. When Ward died, a son of Marshman, and Mack, a young Scotchman from Edinburgh University, joined the missionary partnership. In the half century ending in 1854 this brotherhood had contributed nearly four hundred and fifty thousand dollars to the mission. It held all the property, created by its own energies, in trust on behalf of the Society. The success achieved enabled it to raise large sums which were devoted to missions elsewhere.

When Carey was left the sole survivor of the five who had formed the Society their successors would not continue the work on their plans. Serampore Mission separated from the Society and aided by Christians in various lands carried on Bible translation, opened new evangelizing stations, and established a college to train missionaries and to educate Brahmans and Mohammedans under Christian auspices. The financial burden proved too great, but John Marshman redeemed all their pledges and made over their property to the Society. This he afterwards bought back. He continued his work until 1854, and his successors until 1875.

Before Carey's death, in 1834, the whole Bible

had been translated into forty languages and dialects, and the sacred books of the Hindus into English. Dr. Marshman also translated the Bible into Chinese, prepared a Chinese grammar and dictionary, and translated some of the works of Confucius into English. When the mission press at Serampore was destroyed by fire, in 1812, so great were the interest and enthusiasm at home for the work that £10,000 was raised within fifty days and sent on to Serampore. In 1810 the stations in India were organized into five missions. By 1813 there were twenty stations, with 63 European and native laborers. In 1829 the Serampore College was established under a charter from the Danish government. Among the other results of the labors in India of Carey, Marshman and Ward, and their associates, may be mentioned the first large printing-press, paper mill and steam engine; the first vernacular paper in Bengali; the first savings bank, and the first efforts for the education of native girls and women.

The mission in Ceylon, whose work has been chiefly educational, was opened in 1812. It has stations at Colombo, Ratnapuri and Kandy, with thousands of children in day schools and Sunday-schools.

In 1813 the Society began work in the West Indies, being moved thereto by Moses Baker, a follower of George Liele, a colored man from Georgia, who had formed congregations of slaves at Kingston and other places. After Mr. Liele's death Mr. Baker applied to the Baptist Missionary Society for aid and the Rev. Mr. Rowe was sent out, on the advice of Mr. Wilberforce. In 1817 Rev. James Coultart settled in Kingston, and soon gathered a large and flourishing church. By 1831 there were 14 English missionaries on the island, who had in charge 24 churches, with 10,838 communicants. In that year the slaves rose against their masters; and the missionaries, who had done all in their power to quiet the natives and prevent an insurrection, were arrested and threatened with death, but when brought to trial were acquitted. Some chapels were destroyed by mobs, and Mr. Knibb was sent to England to secure redress. His speeches in favor of the abolition of slavery, awakening a hearty response from the Baptists of England, were instrumental in bringing about that result. The government granted £5,510 for the destroyed chapels, and Christian people added £13,000. The work was renewed, and carried on with such success that in 1842, the jubilee year of the Society, the churches assumed full self-support. The college at Calabar (Kingston), which was opened in 1818, is still maintained.

From 1842 to 1882 the Society carried on a very successful mission on the West Coast of Africa—forming churches, translating books, etc. Owing to the establishment of German colonization on the west coast the mission was transferred to the

Basle Missionary Society in 1880. In 1877 work was begun on the Upper and Lower Congo; and although many deaths have occurred, and the mission premises at Stanley Pool were destroyed by fire in 1886, the work is going forward with much promise.

The Society commenced work in Europe in 1834, and carries it on at present in France, Norway and Italy.

After several attempts it established a mission in China in 1877, which is carrying on vigorous work in Shansi and Shantung. Its work in Japan began in 1879, and its mission to Palestine in 1880.

Its latest statistics show 807 stations; missionaries, 164 men, 114 women; native helpers, 403; communicants, 19,269, this number being less than normal owing largely to disastrous floods in Shantung, North China; 1,790 additions last year; 14,699 pupils under instruction; income in Great Britain, $376,657.

SOCIETY FOR THE PROPAGATION OF THE GOSPEL

The Society for the Propagation of the Gospel in Foreign Parts was chartered in 1701 by King William III. It consisted of 96 members, including the Archbishops of Canterbury and York and the Bishops of London and Ely. The charter defined its purposes to be "receiving, managing and dispensing of funds contributed for the religious instruction of the queen's subjects beyond the seas;

for the maintenance of clergymen in the plantations, colonies and factories of Great Britain, and for the propagation of the gospel in those parts." Its first work was among settlements of English people in Moscow and Archangel, which was soon followed by work in North America, the West Indies and other colonies.

Its first effort at distinctive foreign missionary work was the foundation of a missionary college at Calcutta, in behalf of which a royal letter was issued by the Prince Regent, in 1818, authorizing a general collection, the proceeds of which amounted to £45,747. The original object of this college was to educate native East Indian and European young men for the service of the church. While the working of the college was in some respects unsatisfactory it yielded some good results through the missions which were established under the care of its graduates, and which embraced 113 villages, with 26 chapels and 7 schools. After many disappointments, it is now giving great encouragement in sending forth well-qualified graduates from eight distinct races, in being an effective instrument of Christian education in Bengal, and in promoting evangelistic work in the neighborhood of Calcutta.

The Society opened a mission in Cawnpore in 1841, and in Delhi in 1852, both of which suffered severely in the mutiny of 1857—the Delhi mission being obliterated; but it was reorganized in 1860. In 1877 the University of Cambridge undertook to maintain a body of men who would live and work together in some city in India, and Delhi was fixed upon for the experiment; this Society undertaking the maintenance of most of these Cambridge volunteers.

In 1869 the Society took over the work of Pastor Gossner, of Berlin, in the Chutia Nagpore mission, with 17,000 Kol converts, scattered in 300 villages, which were divided into 35 circles, each with a native "reader" having immediate supervision of the converts, who also had periodical visits from the chief missionary.

In 1835, having taken up some years previously the work of the Christian Knowledge Society in Madras, it constituted a bishopric with its headquarters in that city but embracing the work among the Telugus and that at Tanjore, Tinnevelli, and other centers.

Although the Society began work in Bombay in 1836 it was of little importance until Bishop Douglas, in 1869, laid out a plan for a chain of mission stations, of which Poona, Kolapore and Ahmednuggur were chief. Since that time the work has been very prosperous.

Ceylon was entered in 1838 and Burma in 1859. It has missions also in various portions of the Straits Settlements and in Borneo.

It commenced work in Japan in 1873, in North China in 1874, and in Korea in 1889.

Work in South Africa was begun in 1820, and

includes, as in other countries, both pastoral care of English colonists and evangelistic work among the natives. It now numbers thousands of converts among the Kaffirs and other tribes; and gives much attention to education, and especially to industrial work, teaching the boys carpentry, wagon-making, blacksmithing, tinsmithing, and gardening, and the girls household work. It also has a diocese of Mauritius, including many surrounding islands of the Indian Ocean. It began work in Madagascar in 1864, and set apart a bishop for it in 1874.

The work in Australia, begun in 1795, now has 12 dioceses, two of which are self-supporting. The work in New Zealand, begun in 1837, has six dioceses, independent of England.

That the extreme high-churchism of this Society prevents it from coming into harmony and active co-operation with the great body of Protestant missionary workers is much to be regretted. While there are some notable exceptions, in general its missionaries hold aloof from those of other denominations, and are in marked contrast in this respect with the workers of the Church Missionary Society. The Society for the Propagation of the Gospel reports for 1899, 500 stations; 4,000 outstations; missionaries—611 men, 170 women; 3,326 native helpers; 70,000 communicants; 38,000 pupils under instruction; income in Great Britain, $661,775. The Women's Mission Association reports an income of $41,793.

LONDON MISSIONARY SOCIETY

The London Missionary Society grew out of an invitation sent by Dr. Ryland, a member of the Baptist Missionary Committee, to Dr. David Bogue, a Presbyterian minister, and Mr. Stephen, his friends, to come and listen to the reading of the first letters received from the missionaries Carey and Thomas. With the object of organizing a society for non-Baptists Dr. Bogue wrote an "address to professors of the gospel," exhorting them to earnest prayer and conversation and to consultation in regard to missions to the heathen, and asking an annual subscription to send out twenty or thirty missionaries. This address was published in the *Evangelical Magazine* in September, 1794, and awakened such great interest in England and Scotland that a meeting was agreed upon to provide for the formation of a society on the 4th of November, when ministers of various denominations met, and sent out a circular in January, 1795, proposing the organization of a society. Ministers made known the plan to their congregations, and delegates were appointed to a convention to be held for that purpose in September. A preliminary meeting of ministers was held on the evening of the 20th. On the 21st, in the Spa Fields chapel, Dr. Haweis, of Aldwinkle, preached a stirring sermon on the Great Commission; after which the ministers and laymen adjourned to the "Castle and Falcon," on Aldersgate

(7) 97

street, and formed what was then called "The Missionary Society." The three following days were occupied with missionary meetings in different parts of the city. Christians of all denominations were meeting together, singing the praises of God, joining in hearty prayer for the spread of the gospel, and receiving a baptism of missionary zeal and consecration.

"The Missionary Society" at the outset received much support from Presbyterians and Episcopalians, but gradually they in the main withdrew to work through organizations connected with their own churches, leaving the Society to be carried on mostly by the Independents or Congregationalists; but it still holds to its original declaration: "That its design is not to send Presbyterianism, Independency, Episcopacy, or any other form of church order and government (about which there may be difference of opinion among serious persons), but the glorious gospel of the blessed God to the heathen, and that it shall be left (as it ought to be left) to the minds of the persons whom God may call into the fellowship of his Son from among them to assume for themselves such form of church government as to them shall appear most agreeable to the Word of God." The condition of membership in the Society is an annual payment of one guinea. A general meeting of the Society is held in the month of May in each year, at which directors and officers are elected; and all matters are determined by a majority vote of the members present, The management is by a Board of Directors not more than one third of whom reside in or near London.

In August, 1796, the ship *Duff* with twenty-nine missionaries sailed for Tahiti. In the same year this Society joined with two Scotch societies in sending an expedition to Sierra Leone, which however met with no success. Dr. Vanderkemp and some others were sent to South Africa in December of the same year. A missionary was sent to Calcutta in 1798, but the mission in India was not definitely organized until 1804, when Messrs. Ringeltaube, Cran and DesGranges were stationed at Vizagapatam and Travancore, and Mr. Voss at Colombo, Ceylon. The North India Mission was established in 1816. Some help was sent to the West Indies in 1807, which resulted in founding a mission at Demarara, which was afterward extended to British Guiana and to Jamaica. The mission to Mauritius was opened in 1814, and in 1818 the work in Madagascar began, which had a career of wonderful success and whose history is among the most interesting of all missionary annals. In the same year work was opened in Siberia and Tartary; but it was closed by a Russian edict in 1840.

Robert Morrison, the first of a noble line of missionaries to China, was sent out in 1807, and was obliged to come to New York to secure passage, owing to the opposition of the East India Company to the beginning of missionary work in China.

In subsequent years the missions thus opened were reinforced and strengthened from time to time, but no new work was opened until 1879, when the Society responded to a call from the Dark Continent and established a mission at Lake Tanganyika, made sacred by the memories of Livingstone.

This Society, like the American Board of Commissioners for Foreign Missions, gradually lost its interdenominational character. The Church Missionary Society, formed in 1799, took off the evangelical churchmen. In 1814 the Wesleyan Methodist Society was organized, and later the Presbyterian societies drew off that element of the constituency; for many years it has been almost wholly sustained by Congregationalists or Independents. It has been a great pioneer society, a leader in the South Sea, in China, in Africa and Madagascar. Its roll contains many of the most eminent names in missionary history, such as those of John Williams, of Erromanga; Robert Morrison and William H. Medhurst of China; John Vanderkemp, Robert and Mary Moffat and David Livingstone, of Africa. At first many of the missionaries sent out were artisans, without scholastic training; but this mistake was not long continued, and in later years the missionaries of this Society have been noted for scholarly attainments as well as for consecrated service.

The latest statistics of the London Missionary Society show 97 stations; 1,260 outstations; missionaries—196 men, 226 women; 5,240 native helpers; 52,803 communicants, of whom 1,817 were added last year; 50,613 pupils under instruction; income in Great Britain, $666,526.

CHURCH MISSIONARY SOCIETY

The Church Missionary Society owes its origin to a meeting of sixteen clergymen at the "Castle and Falcon," London, April 16, 1799, who organized the "Society for Missions to Africa and the East;" its object being to take the gospel to Mohammedans and heathen, the Society for the Propagation of the Gospel having sent missionaries only to British colonies. In 1812 it changed its name to "The Church Missionary Society for Africa and the East," in order to indicate its connection with the established church, but distinctly avowed its purpose to maintain friendly intercourse with other Protestant Societies engaged in the same work; and it has ever remained "remarkable not only for this brotherly co-operation and honor, but also for its evangelical large-heartedness, its sound principles of method and its excellent government and organization at home and abroad." It is conducted by a Patron, always a member of the Royal Family; a Vice Patron, the Archbishop of Canterbury; a President, who must be a layman; a Vice President, usually a clergyman, and a committee of twenty-four laymen and all the clergymen who have been for one year or more members of the Society.

Its first missionaries were sent to West Africa, and the foundations of the work in Sierra Leone were laid in 1816. Work began in New Zealand in 1814, in the Levant in 1815, in India in 1816, in Ceylon in 1817; work among the North American Indians in 1826, in East Africa in 1844, in China in 1845, in Mauritius in 1854, and in Japan in 1869. This also has been a great pioneer Society, especially in Africa, America and New Zealand; and has been particularly active in work among Mohammedans. Its income is usually more than that of any other Society, and it has had a notable list of workers—prominent among whom are Selwyn, Hannington, Mackay, Crowther, French, Burden and Moule. Since 1887 it has sent out all properly qualified candidates, without regard to the state of its finances, and it has been remarkably successful in following this policy.

Statistics of the Church Missionary Society for 1899 show 520 stations; missionaries—530 men, 383 women; native helpers, 6,154; communicants, 64,904, of whom 493 were added last year; pupils under instruction, 88,094; income in Great Britain, $1,889,135. The Church of England Zenana Missionary Society, a woman's organization which acts in harmony with the Church Missionary Society, reports 72 stations; 221 missionaries; 850 native helpers; 10,468 pupils under instruction; income in Great Britain, $230,575.

WESLEYAN MISSIONARY SOCIETY

The Wesleyan Methodist movement was of a missionary character from its very inception. As early as 1744, through the efforts of Whitefield, special hours of prayer were observed for the outpouring of the Spirit on Christendom, and upon the "whole inhabited earth." John Wesley's first visit to America was for the purpose of preaching to the Indians. In 1786 Thomas Coke, providentially driven out of his course to Nova Scotia, landed in the British West Indies, and a mission to the negro slaves was at once commenced. He had the charge of Wesleyan Missions until 1804, when a Committee of three was appointed to oversee the work. A mission to West Africa was undertaken in 1811; and on Dec. 31, 1813, Dr. Coke, at the age of 76, sailed for Ceylon to found the third Methodist mission. He died on his way thither, and found a watery grave, but the Wesleyan Methodist Mission was organized and has grandly carried on its work. It is managed by a Committee appointed annually by the Wesleyan Methodist Conference, which also elects its general secretaries and treasurers.

The Society followed up its work in West Africa by entering South Africa in 1814, New South Wales in 1815, Tasmania in 1821, Victoria in 1838, Queensland in 1850 and China in 1853. Its work among the Maoris of New Zealand was begun in 1822, in the Friendly Islands in 1826, and its most remarkable and successful work in the Fiji Islands in 1834. Of this the *Cyclopedia of Missions* well says: "There is nothing more wonderful than the transformation of these savages through the power of the gospel, nothing more touching than their readiness to receive and their eagerness to make known that gospel to those who know it not."

The mission to New Britain was an outgrowth of the Fiji mission. In 1875 nine of the native preachers volunteered to go on this dangerous mission. Seven of them were married, and their wives gladly joined in their offer. The English consul set before them the great hazard of their undertaking, to which they replied: "We are all of one mind. We know what those islands are. We have given ourselves to this work. If we get killed, well; if we live, well. We have had everything explained to us, and we know the danger. We are willing to go." Four of this party were treacherously murdered and eaten by cannibals. After this had happened one of the wives in a new outgoing party was asked whether she still purposed to go to such a field, and replied: "I am like the outrigger of a canoe—where the canoe goes there you will find the outrigger." In 1888 their first missionary meetings were held, and £50 contributed to the Wesleyan Missionary Society. The work is now very prosperous.

Work was commenced in China in 1852 by the Rev. George Piercy, who went out at his own expense but was afterward accepted by the Society and appointed to Canton. This has developed into a very important work in this portion of Southern China.

Statistics for 1899 give 276 stations; 320 outstations; 182 missionaries; 180 native helpers; 46,262 communicants, of whom 1,622 were added last year; 90,117 pupils under instruction; income in Great Britain, $557,901. The "Women's Auxiliary" reports 44 stations; 300 outstations; 52 missionaries; 140 native helpers; 18,254 pupils under instruction; income in Great Britain, $66,927.

ENGLISH PRESBYTERIAN SOCIETY

The Presbyterian Church of England sent out the Rev. William C. Burns, as its first missionary to China, in 1847. He labored for four years in Hong Kong, Canton, and the neighborhood, but in 1851 proceeded to Amoy, where Dr. James Young was his medical colleague. In succeeding years many excellent missionaries were sent out, prominent among whom were the Rev. David Sandeman and the Rev. Carstairs Douglas. Their three great fields in China are at Amoy, Swatow, and in the Hakka country. They also have a flourishing mission on the Island of Formosa. Their missionaries have worked in great harmony with those of the Reformed Church of America, and churches have been organized, and a Presbytery constituted from those attached to both missions. The missions of this church are among the most successful of all engaged in the work in China.

Latest reports of the Presbyterian Church in England show 75 stations; 120 outstations; missionaries—35 men, 49 women; 156 native helpers; 5,943 communicants, of whom 477 were added last year; income in Great Britain, $117,985.

SCOTCH PRESBYTERIAN SOCIETY

The Presbyterian Church of Scotland may justly date the beginning of its missionary efforts, from 1699, when four missionaries were sent out to the Scotch colony at Darien to supply the vacant places of two ministers who went out with the colonists, and who had died. In 1825 the General Assembly appointed its first Foreign Mission Committee, consisting of ten able men. The departure of Alexander Duff for Calcutta in 1829 greatly stimulated the missionary ardor of the church. The seminary commenced by Dr. Duff in 1830 became a great educational institution in which all the instruction was brought to bear on the religious well-being of the students. The high quality of its education broke down the prejudices of many Hindus against its religious teachings, and it has proved itself a great power in the progress of Christianity in India.

In 1835 the General Assembly took over the work of the old Scottish Missionary Society which had been founded in 1822. Drs. John Wilson and J. Murray Mitchell and other laborers had been trying since 1828 to do the same kind of work in Bombay and Poona that Dr. Duff was doing in Calcutta. The transfer of the mission developed the English school at Bombay into a missionary college, where the first Parsee converts were brought to Christ, and many educated Brahmans were won over to faith in Christianity. Among these the names of Rev. Dhanjibhai Naoroji, a Parsee, and Rev. Narayan Sheshadri, are reckoned as those of two of the most efficient and successful of native ministers.

Dr. Duff's stirring appeal in the General Assembly of 1837 led to the founding of the mission in Madras by the Rev. John Anderson, which has been very successful.

The disruption of the Church of Scotland occurred in 1843, since which time we must reckon both the Established and the Free Church of Scotland among the great missionary factors of the century. The Established Church had much property in India, but nearly all the missionaries went into the Free Church. The Established Church carried on its institutions and its work in the presidencies of Calcutta, Bombay and Madras, giving much attention to the work of higher education. A mission in the Punjab was opened in 1857. Its mission in Gujerat has been very successful, though at the outset one of the missionaries, the Rev. Thomas Hunter, his wife and infant child were shot at the time of the mutiny. Missionaries were sent to Darjeeling in 1870 who have since been reinforced, and much good work is in hand.

Work was begun in Africa in 1874, growing out of the news of Livingstone's death and Mr. Stanley's letter from Uganda; and in 1877 a mission was started at Ichang, in the interior of China. The Society also has Jewish missions in Egypt, Beirut, Constantinople and other regions. It has many excellent workers, and is recognized as one of the great missionary agencies of our time.

Church of Scotland statistics show 21 stations; 77 outstations; European missionaries—44 men, 85 women; 537 native helpers; 2,334 communicants, of whom 251 were added last year; 5,957 pupils under instruction, income in Great Britain, $188,035. The Women's Association reports income in Great Britain, $71,624.

THE METHODIST NEW CONNEXION MISSIONARY SOCIETY

This is the oldest of the divisions of Wesleyan Methodism in England, having been organized in 1797. Its attention was early called to the needs of Ireland and Canada, and it began a mission in Ireland in 1825 and one in Canada in 1835. Its heathen mission was established in China in 1859. Work was begun in Shanghai and subsequently removed to Tientsin, in North China. This is the only foreign mission the denomination has. A strong native agency has been developed in connection with the mission, and it has been the policy of the society to raise up a force of native teachers and preachers.

A farmer from a distant town came to the chapel service in Tientsin one day and remained at the after meeting, where he said he had come to the city in obedience to a dream. He became a convert, and on his return to his own neighborhood began a gospel work which led to a great awakening and a new center of Christian influence was established.

IRISH PRESBYTERIAN FOREIGN MISSIONS

The Presbyterian Church of Ireland was organized in 1840, and one of the first things it did was to call upon two men to go out to India to form a mission. They had not offered to go, but the Church deemed it had a right to ask them to go, and it was set down as a precedent for all time to come. Besides the India work, with its seven stations in the Gujerat district, the Church has a mission in Manchuria, China, with stations at Newchang, Kinchan, and Kirin, and missions among the Jews. It has in all 19 stations and 1,960 communicants. Its income in 1899 was nearly $101,000

FOREIGN MISSIONS OF THE WELSH CALVINISTIC PRESBYTERIAN CHURCH

The Calvinistic Presbyterians or Methodists began to contribute to the London Missionary Society soon after it was established. In 1840 it established a missionary society of its own. Its first field was in Bengal, India. The work there covers seven districts, and is chiefly in the hills. The second mission was begun in Brittany, France, in 1842. The Society received $46,839 in 1898, when it reported 3,231 communicants in its two fields.

THE PRIMITIVE METHODIST MISSIONARY SOCIETY

The Missionary Society organized by the Primitive Methodists of England, dating from 1843, was for many years engaged in home and colonial work only.

It planted churches of its order in Australia, New Zealand and Canada. In 1870 it sent two missionaries to the Spanish Island of Fernando Po. A devoted Primitive Methodist captain and carpenter of a trading vessel had become interested in the people during a brief stay at the island, and induced the Society to take steps to evangelize the people, some of whom were Baptists. The mission has grown despite determined Roman Catholic opposition.

A second mission, at Aliwal, in Cape Colony, was begun in 1870. It is among the natives. In 1889 missionaries were sent out to establish a mission on the Zambesi River. The Society has 1,256 communicants in connection with its foreign missions, and raises about $35,000 a year for their support.

SOUTH AMERICAN MISSIONARY SOCIETY

The history of the founding of this Society partakes largely of the heroic if not the romantic in missions. Captain Allen Gardiner, its founder, was a man of means who was thoroughly devoted to the cause of missions. With his wife and family he visited many countries with the object of finding the "most abandoned heathen" on earth and becoming a pioneer Christian missionary to them. Finally, he settled on the natives of South America as, at all events, sufficiently "abandoned" for his purpose and tried to reach some of the mountain tribes, but his efforts were frustrated by the Roman Catholic priesthood. Then he turned his attention to Patagonia, where the Church of Rome was not represented, and in 1844 he organized the "Patagonian Missionary Society." Soon after he and a few others attempted to establish a mission in Tierra del Fuego, without success. The Society was discouraged, but Captain Gardiner was determined to persevere. He seems to have been formed for the purpose of battling with adverse circumstances. A thousand pounds was raised, of which nearly a third was given by Captain Gardiner himself, and in 1850 he started again, with a surgeon, a carpenter, three Cornish fishermen and one other—all devoted Christian men who realized the desperate nature of their venture. They were left with their boats in a harbor of Tierra del

Fuego, on which they were to live because of the violent and thieving nature of the people. Nine months of misfortune and disaster followed, scarcely equaled in the annals of Arctic exploration. In a heavy storm they lost an anchor and both of their small boats for landing. Then they discovered that the supply of powder and shot, which they were to use to supply themselves with game and defend themselves from the natives, had by some oversight gone on to San Francisco in the ship which brought them. Another storm destroyed one of their two vessels. With the remaining vessel they made another harbor, where they all finally perished. The relief expedition arrived too late, and only found the remains of two of the men, including Captain Gardiner, and their journals.

The details of the sufferings and death of these heroic missionaries did what Gardiner could not do while he was living, roused a strong interest in South American missionary effort. The Society was re-formed, as the South American Missionary Society, on Mr. Gardiner's plan, with one of the West Falkland Islands as a station, whence communication could be had with Tierra del Fuego. Another attempt was made in 1856, with success. Fuegians were induced to come to the Falklands, a few at a time, and there received Christian instruction, and at the same time imparted a knowledge of the Fuegian tongue to the missionaries.

The Society has work not only among the Fuegians and other natives of South America, but in accordance with Captain Gardiner's plan has missions to English and to Spanish- and Portuguese-speaking peoples. Missions on the East Coast are in Argentina, Uruguay, Paraguay and Brazil, on the West Coast in Chili.

The income of the Society is about $56,000 a year. It is supported by Church of England people.

THE FRIENDS' FOREIGN MISSIONARY ASSOCIATION

The Friends of England claim a long and consistent record as friends of foreign missions. In the days of George Fox they sent missionaries to China and to Prester John's country, and on subsequent occasions Friends have done mission work in foreign fields. In 1865 a provisional committee was appointed to promote the cause, and in the following year the first missionary was sent to India. The association now has missions in India, Madagascar and China. Industrial schools, day schools, zenana visitation, evangelistic and medical work are carried on by the missionaries. The Friends of England also maintain a medical mission in Constantinople, and a Syrian mission for the education of boys and girls. In the latter, the Friends of New England bear an important part.

NORTH AFRICAN MISSION

Algeria being open, under French occupation, to the reception of the gospel, attention was at-

tracted to the field, in England, by the visits of
George Pearce, Mr. H. Grattan Guinness and
others, 1876-1880, and a committee was formed
for the conduct of a mission among the Kabyles.
The movement is undenominational. The mission
was begun in 1881, but its progress was slow
owing to the great difficulties encountered, particularly with representatives of the French Government. There are stations not only in Algiers, but
also in Morocco, Tunis, Tripoli, North Arabia.
The work is among the Berbers, the Bedouins and
other Moslem tribes.

CONGO BALOLO MISSION

This is an undenominational mission established
in 1889 by Mr. and Mrs. H. Grattan Guinness, of the
East London Institute. Its sphere of operations
is in the Balolo country, said to have a population
of ten millions all of whom speak the same language.
The country extends beyond Equatorville on the
south side of the Congo. This mission is a part
of the work formerly under the direction of the
Guinnesses, the rest having been transferred to the
American Baptist Missionary Union.

UNITED METHODIST FREE CHURCHES MISSIONARY SOCIETY

The United Methodist Free Churches are the
result of a union of the Wesleyan Association with
a number of churches of the Wesleyan Reform,

in 1857. The Missionary Society of the united body inherited missions in Jamaica and Australia. It has since then opened missions in Sierra Leone, West Africa, where it has a considerable body of native communicants, and in East Africa, among the Wa Nyika race, dwelling about twelve miles from the coast of the Indian Ocean. The renowned African missionary, Dr. Krapf, assisted in founding this enterprise. Attempts have been made also to reach the Gallas. The mission has suffered severely from loss of missionaries by disease and violence.

The Society has a mission in China, with headquarters at Ningpo.

The Society has an income of about $50,000. It has 8,651 communicants on its foreign fields, a number exceeded by few societies in Great Britain and Ireland.

UNIVERSITIES' MISSION TO CENTRAL AFRICA

This mission was the result of appeals by David Livingstone and Bishop Gray of Cape Town. Archdeacon Mackenzie, of Natal, was consecrated Bishop for the mission which was established by him at Magomero, south of Lake Nyassa, at the suggestion of Dr. Livingstone, among a colony of released slaves. The site proved unhealthy, and Bishop Tozer, the successor of Bishop Mackenzie, removed it to Zanzibar, where released slaves were carefully trained. After some years a chain of stations was formed from the coast to Lake Nyassa, and the headquarters of the mission removed to Lukama, on the Lake.

The mission is supported by members of the Church of England. Its income in 1898 was somewhat less than $160,000.

BRITISH AND FOREIGN BIBLE SOCIETY

This Society was organized in London in 1804, on an undenominational basis, to furnish the Scriptures to populations in the home field, in the colonies and in other countries, whether Christian, Mohammedan or pagan. The first foreign branch of the society was in Nuremberg, a Roman Catholic priest distributing the first consignment of 1,000 copies in Suabia. The first foreign edition was of John's Gospel in Mohawk and English. The Society was especially successful in inducing various European countries to organize Bible societies of their own. It entered the various mission fields of Asia, Africa, North and South America, and the islands of the sea, and furnished the Scriptures or portions of the Scriptures to missionary tribes and peoples in their own tongue. It maintains many agencies for Bible distribution, and as long ago as 1868 its income passed the million mark.

FREE CHURCH OF SCOTLAND

The Free Church of Scotland began work in 1843 with the advantage of having a mission and a number of missionaries in India. Giving up the buildings to the Established Church, however, it became necessary to purchase new premises and erect new buildings; but these were speedily provided by generous contributions, and the school in Calcutta opened with a larger number of pupils than ever.

In 1864 the congregation at Calcutta opened a branch mission among the Santhals, in Upper Bengal, and established schools at three other places. The schools at Bombay, Poona and Madras were also carried on successfully. In due time the Madras school became the United Christian College for all South India. The medical missions at Madras and Conjeveram have been very useful in educating native youth as physicians and nurses.

In 1844 the Free Church took over the Kaffir missions from the Glasgow Missionary Society and opened a mission in the Nagpur province, in the center of India, under Rev. Stephen S. Hislop, who found three excellent laymen, survivors of the German Missions, who were a great help to him. Rev. Robert Hunter inaugurated a second station at Kampti. Institutions were established, the chief of which was the Hislop Missionary College. In 1864 the Rev. Narayan Sheshadri, a graduate of Wilson College, under the Established Church, founded the Deccan Mission in the Mohammedan state of Hyderabad. All the colleges are affiliated with universities, and train Christian converts for service, both in vernacular and English preaching, as Presbyterian pastors and missionaries.

The Kaffir mission was begun by the Glasgow Missionary Society, which sent out Rev. W. R. Thompson and a catechist in 1821. They began at a small village on the Chumic river, and baptized five Kaffirs in June, 1823. In December of that year the Rev. John Ross and wife arrived to reinforce the mission. A church, a printing press and schools soon made a great change in the habits of the natives and awakened a desire for education. New stations were established at several churches, and when the mission was handed over to the Free Church, in 1844, the work was in a prosperous condition; with a missionary seminary, valued at about $12,500, with 14 theological students, and some graduates already engaged in evangelistic work. The work continued to grow under the new administration until the war of 1846 compelled the missionaries to flee—some returning to Scotland, and others going to labor among the colonists at Cape Town. On the restoration of peace, in 1848, the missionaries returned to their posts, the seminary was reopened, destroyed property was gradually replaced, and in a few years the mission was moving successfully in all departments.

The mission has been divided into two, known as the South and North Kaffir missions, divided by the great Kei river. In the Lovedale Institution, at Alice, of which Rev. J. Stewart, M.D., is in charge, the boys are taught farming, carpentering, wagon making, printing and bookbinding, while the girls are instructed in domestic arts, and all receive a good general education and are taught the word of God. There is a prosperous church at Lovedale, out of which a number of other churches have grown.

The North Kaffir mission has its center at Blythewood, with a good institution, and does its work mainly among the Fingoes. At its jubilee, in 1871, 2,000 natives and 1,000 Europeans joined in thanksgiving to God. The one station of Kaffir huts had grown into 10 great evangelistic centers with over 70 outstations.

Dr. Duff's appeals, after his visit to South Africa, led to the establishment of a mission among the Zulu Kaffirs of Natal in 1867—the first stations occupied being Pietermaritzburg and Impolweni, under the Rev. James Allison, a most devoted missionary. The Rev. John Bruce, Rev. James Scott and many other faithful laborers followed. In 1874 the Dowager Countess of Aberdeen made a large gift to establish a memorial station in honor of her son, the Hon. J. H. Gordon. This was established in Natal, near the border of Zululand, and the Rev. J. Dalzell became the efficient missionary in charge.

But perhaps the most interesting field of this church is East Central Africa, which was opened under the appeals of Livingstone. It was named the Livingstone Mission and purposed to occupy the country around Lake Nyassa. The first settlement was made at Cape Maclean, at the south end of the lake, by the Rev. James Stewart, C.E., whose life was sacrificed, and he was succeeded by the Rev. Robert Laws. From this center many places were occupied along the west shore of Nyassa, in North and South Angoniland, between lakes Nyassa and Tanganyika, and in the uplands southwest of Cape Maclean. Dr. Laws gained the confidence of the people, and gathered large numbers of children into schools. The mission has passed through some trying periods, but has met with much success and is well sustained.

The Free Church commenced work in Syria in 1872, after a visit by Dr. Duff and Principal Lumsden to the mountains of Lebanon. They sent out Rev. John Rae and united with the work of the Lebanon Schools Society, which had been carried on since 1839. They occupied Shevier as their first station, and followed with a number of out-stations. A Syrian evangelical church has been formed and a church building erected.

This Church has also done a great work in the New Hebrides, in connection with other Presbyterian Boards of Scotland, Canada, Australia and New Zealand. The work began in Aneityum, where John Geddie labored successfully and translated portions of the Scriptures. He began in 1848, and in six years there were 30 schools and 2,600 people attended public worship. A memorial tablet in the church at Anelgahat says: "When he landed in 1848 there were no Christians here, and when he died in 1872 there were no heathen."

In Fotuna John Williams succeeded in conciliating the people but his death prevented the sending out of teachers. Some of the Samoan teachers sent in 1841 were killed and eaten, but in the face of persecution the work has been carried on with a good degree of success, and a medical mission has also been established. In Aniwa, in spite of the killing of some of the early teachers from Aneityum in 1840 and succeeding years, the work has prospered, and in 1866 J. G. Paton found a people prepared to listen to his teachings. The mission house was erected on a site which had been devoted to cannibal feasts. In eight years the island was completely Christianized.

Tanna was a very trying field for many years. The native teachers of John Williams were obliged to flee; and Turner and Nesbit, of the London Missionary Society, barely escaped with their lives in 1843. From that time until 1858 Samoan teachers tried to introduce the gospel in the midst of severe opposition. In the latter year John Paton and Mr. Copeland landed on the island and were soon joined by others; and in later years the mission has been very successful. Erromanga is known for the martyrdom of Williams and of others who followed him. Rev. G. N. Gordon, of Nova Scotia, went out in 1857, and did much effective work for four years, but he and his wife were murdered in 1861, the superstitions of the natives having been awakened by a series of calamities. His brother, J. D. Gordon, succeeded him in 1864, and Mr. J. McNair followed in 1868. Mr. Gordon was treacherously murdered by a native in 1872. Here also the gospel has won many trophies in recent years. The New Hebrides Mission Synod has supreme authority in all general ecclesiastical matters.

Work in South Arabia was commenced in 1885 by the Hon. Ion and Mrs. Keith-Falconer, who settled at Sheik-Othwan for work among Mohammedans and Somalis in the neighborhood of Aden. The Committee of the Free Church agreed to appoint Dr. B. Stewart Cowan as a medical missionary in 1886, but the mission is conducted as undenominational. Hon. Ion Keith-Falconer died in 1887, and was buried in the cemetery of Aden Camp, but immediately thereafter the Countess Dowager of Kintore and Mrs. Keith-Falconer each guaranteed £300 a year for the support of two missionaries, and in a few years the mission was fully equipped. Progress, though slow, is not without encouragement.

The statistics of the Free Church show 45 stations; 304 out-stations; missionaries—127 men, 135 women; 1,149 native helpers; 10,977 communicants, of whom 395 were added last year; 35,298 pupils under instruction; income in Great Britain, $254,570. The Women's Society reports an income of $79,680.

UNITED PRESBYTERIAN CHURCH

The United Presbyterian Church of Scotland was formed in 1847 from bodies that had seceded from the Established Church and were known as the "Secession Church" and the "Relief Church." Missionaries were sent out from Scotland early in this century by the Scottish Missionary Society and the Glasgow Missionary Society. The first Scotch missionary to the heathen was Peter Greig, who went to South Africa, and who belonged to one of the churches which formed the United Presbyterian Church.

Its work has been in the West Indies, where it took up the mission which had been opened by Rev. George Blyth and others of the Scottish Missionary Society, followed in 1835 by Rev. James Paterson and others of the United Secession Church. Stations were opened and vigorous missionary work was carried on in Jamaica and surrounding regions, and in 1846 the negroes had been raised from their degradation, and were already sending out missionaries to West Africa. The work has continued to be successful. There are about 50 ordained ministers, about half of whom are natives, and over 12,000 members. Trinidad was entered in 1835 by Rev. Alexander Kennedy, and the work has been prosecuted with increasing success until the present time.

The work of this society in Africa has centered

at two stations: 1. Old Calabar, where the Rev. H. M. Waddell and other missionaries were sent by the Jamaica Negroes in 1846, and found the kings and people somewhat civilized, with considerable knowledge of English. The printing press was soon introduced and the Bible translated, and the work has been maintained with much success. 2. Kaffraria, where work was begun by the Glasgow Missionary Society a portion of which came under the Free Church, in 1844, and the remainder under the United Presbyterian Church in 1847. The ravages of war have interfered with mission work, but the ground has been held until over 3,000 members have been received into the churches.

In India this Church has carried on work in Rajpootana and its feudatory states since 1860, and has been very prosperous. The self-denying labors of William and Gavin Martin during the famine of 1869 had a wonderful effect upon the people, and gave them great confidence in the missionaries. A mission press is established at Ajmere, and the work is constantly growing.

In China, Manchuria has been the field of labor —first by a medical missionary at Ningpo, and after 1870 by Rev. Dr. Alexander Williamson at Chefoo. Rev. John Ross and Rev. John Macintyre began the work in Manchuria in 1873, and the entire mission was concentrated in that field in 1885, where it has met with a large measure of success.

The Church sent out its first missionaries to

Japan in 1863. It united with other bodies of Presbyterian polity in forming the "Church of Christ in Japan," which has had a rapid growth, and carries on very effective educational and evangelistic work.

Statistics of the United Presbyterian Church show 114 stations; 268 out-stations; European missionaries—93 men, 43 women; 881 native helpers; 26,971 communicants; 21,070 pupils under instruction; income in Scotland, $305,186.

CHINA INLAND MISSION

This Society was formed in England in response to appeals of Mr. J. Hudson Taylor for the unoccupied provinces of the great Chinese Empire, particularly the inland provinces. Mr. Taylor had spent several years in missionary work in China, having been sent out by the Chinese Evangelization Society. After some years of service he separated from that Society because of difference in views, but continued his work independently. He returned to England in 1860, impressed with the feeling that the great need of China could not be met unless a large force of evangelists could be put into the field. He sent out several young men in the next few years to labor on this plan, their expenses only being provided. He published a little book in which the needs of China were set forth so convincingly that a society was formed, and he himself with several volunteers sailed for the field in 1866. At first the home organization was exceedingly simple; one man acted as treasurer and printed an occasional paper. Then a small council was formed and honorary secretaries did the necessary work. Later a resident secretary was appointed, and the staff was gradually increased as the work grew.

The first stations in China were in the provinces of Chekiang, Kiang-su, Ngan-hwuy, and Kiang-si. At the end of the first ten years there were 44 missionaries, including their wives, assisted by 70 native helpers and six Bible women. In 1886, when the Mission had been in operation twenty years, it had stations in eleven provinces not one of which had any Protestant missions in 1865, before the society began its labors, and in seven other provinces. The number of its missionaries was 152, not including wives. As the occupation of new stations was apt to be accompanied with riotous attacks upon the missionaries the plan of visiting a place several times before occupying it was adopted, to allow the people to become familiar with the missionaries. The result was, it is said, quite satisfactory.

The Mission, according to its latest reports, has 149 stations and 169 out-stations, with 323 male and 450 female missionaries, and 605 native helpers. The number of communicants is 7,147. The annual income of the society is about $190,000.

On arrival in the field new workers are sent to one of the training schools maintained by the Mission, and are there prepared for their work, serving as probationers. From the training school they go to a station and continue their studies under direction of the senior missionaries. A course of study divided into six sections is laid down. If all goes well, and the probationer gives promise of usefulness, he is accepted at the end of two years as a junior missionary, and becomes assistant to a missionary on a district. At the end of five years he is eligible to appointment as a senior missionary if he passes the examinations satisfactorily. Several districts are grouped under the supervision of a superintendent who may call the senior missionaries of his district together at any time for counsel. The superintendents are members of the general council of the Mission, which has quarterly conferences. No promise of salary is made to the missionaries, many of whom are possessed of sufficient means of their own or are supported by friends. The treasurer in China receives remittances from time to time from London and Toronto and supplies the needs of those who have no other provision, the funds being divided *pro rata*. Sometimes the funds are inadequate, in which case the missionaries have to get along as best they can.

The Mission is supported by voluntary contributions, no personal solicitations or collections being made. Among the supporters are members of various denominations. The direction of the work is solely in the hands of the missionaries on the field.

OTHER SOCIETIES IN GREAT BRITAIN

There are many other societies in England and Scotland which are interested either directly or indirectly in foreign missions. Some are small and have no particular history. There are sixteen foreign missionary societies, besides those already described, fourteen colonial and continental societies, three medical missions, seven tract and Bible societies, and thirteen missions to the Jews. The aggregate receipts of all these societies in 1898 were over $1,000,000.

The combined statistics of the Protestant Missionary Societies of Great Britain, as given in the *Almanac of Missions* for 1900, published by the American Board of Commissioners for Foreign Missions, are as follows: 3,370 stations; 7,565 outstations; European missionaries—2,816 men, 2,557 women; 22,191 native helpers; 372,195 communicants; 13,278 added last year; 448,362 pupils under instruction; income in Great Britain, $7,766,740.

CHAPTER VIII

CONTINENTAL MISSIONARY SOCIETIES

BASLE MISSIONARY SOCIETY

THIS is the oldest of the missionary societies of Germany, excepting, of course, the Moravian Church. The Society was formed in 1815 for the special purpose of training men for missionary service in Basle. Before that they had for some years received their training in Berlin. When ready for service these students generally offered themselves to London or Holland Societies. In 1821 the Society sent two men to Southern Russia, and thus entered directly upon missionary work. Missions in Liberia and on the Gold Coast in West Africa, and on the west coast of India were undertaken in the same decade. Subsequently, China and Cameroon, Africa, were added to the Society's fields. Those who managed its affairs had a difficult undertaking. It was by no means regarded as a necessary or desirable enterprise, and it was the policy of its successive inspectors or directors to extend constantly the circle of its friends and supporters. Its methods are those usual in foreign missionary fields, —evangelistic, educational, medical, etc. It also has been interested in industrial movements. It has provided lands for tillage, shops, and other industrial resources for the training and employment of the natives. This feature necessitated the establishment of commercial houses on the Gold Coast and in India to manage the products of the various industries. The trade department has proved remunerative, furnishing about 17 per cent of the income. This industrial development is made possible by the fact that the men trained at the Mission House in Basle are almost invariably from the laboring classes. Of all those who entered up to 1882 only 17 were without a vocation. Of the 1,112 men 143 were farmers, 98 weavers, 69 shoemakers, 65 workers in wood, 50 workers in iron, 73 teachers, etc. Every student must have a trade. In every field, therefore, there are skilled farmers, mechanics, and artisans of various classes.

The Society is undenominational, and has affiliations with members of most of the Protestant churches of Central Europe. Its affairs are under the control of a Board of seven laymen and six ministers. The Board is self-perpetuating. No specific salary is offered to missionaries; but they are told that they will receive necessary care. The Board exercises a direct supervision over them, not only as to their service but also as to their state in life. They are not expected to marry without the approval of the Board. Homes in Basle are maintained for the children of missionaries. As to the churches in the field, the Presbyterian form of organization is employed and a simple ritual is used.

The receipts of the Society exceed $250,000 a year.

BERLIN MISSIONARY SOCIETY

The Berlin Society, strictly the Society for the Promotion of Evangelical Missions among the Heathen, grew out of the school established by Pastor Jänicke in Berlin for the training of missionaries. In this school missionary candidates from Basle were prepared for the work before the Basle Society was formed. The Berlin Society dates from 1824, but the previous years were years of preparation for the organization, which was brought about at a meeting in which the great German theologian, Tholuck, and the eminent Church historian, Neander, were leading spirits. At first the purpose of the Society was to raise funds to help other societies, but in a few years it decided to enter the field itself.

The business of the Society is in the hands of a self-perpetuating committee of eighteen. The administrator is called Director. The Seminary in Berlin for the training of missionaries is an important feature of home management. Applicants must have a good common-school education, and must spend a year in Berlin in preparation for admission. In this period their Christian character, knowledge of the Bible and general fitness for missionary work is tested. As the candidates are largely of the working classes, theological instruction, based on the Lutheran standards, is given in the

Seminary. The course of study extends over four years. The income of the Society is in the neighborhood of $100,000. In establishing a mission station the usual plan is to secure property large enough to accommodate the necessary mission buildings and also houses for the native converts; mission families or communities thus being established.

The two fields of the Society are Africa and China. In Africa there are stations in the Orange Free State, the Transvaal, Cape Colony, Kaffraria and Natal, and there are six synods in the field. In connection with these synods are between 20,000 and 25,000 communicants.

The mission in China was begun in 1882, or rather received in that year from the Barmen Society. It is in the city of Canton.

FOREIGN MISSIONS OF THE MORAVIANS

The Moravians have never been a numerous sect, but they have always been an intensely active missionary body. Their zeal for the conversion of the heathen has never been surpassed, indeed has scarcely been equaled by that of any other Christian people. The name given them, Moravians, from the country of Moravia, in Germany, is not their official title. They call themselves Moravians, in common with the rest of the world, but their organization is officially the *Unitas Fratrum.* The Moravians go back to the fifteenth century for their origin.

The followers of John Huss, the Bohemian re-- former and martyr, were brethren of the same or- der and doctrine. They were suppressed just before the Thirty Years' War, but they preserved their episcopate until opportunity came to renew the Brotherhood on the estate of Count Zinzendorf, in Saxony. Here the town of Herrnhut was founded, and there the brethren lived as a community. When Moravians came to the United States they founded the town of Bethlehem, Penn., on the same plan. The Church owned the lands and stocked the farms, the industrial establishments, etc., and they were worked for its benefit. In return the Church provided the inhabitants with the necessaries of life. Whoever had private means retained them. This policy was given up more than fifty years ago in the United States but was retained in a modified form in Germany.

Count Zinzendorf became interested in foreign missions very early in his youth, while he was a stu- dent in the Academy of Halle. He fell in with men who were being prepared to go to the Malabars in India, in connection with a Danish mission, and during a visit in Copenhagen listened with intense interest to an account of the condition of Negroes in St. Thomas, West Indies. He related these things to the Brethren on his return to Herrnhut, and two young men offered to go to St. Thomas as missionaries. In 1732 one of these young men, together with Bishop David Nitschmann, set out for the West Indies. This was the beginning of Moravian missions.

The Church in Germany, Great Britain and the United States is one, and foreign missions are directed by the Church itself through its General Synod, composed of representatives from the three provinces, Germany, Great Britain and the United. States, and from the foreign missions. The General Synod meets once in ten or twelve years and appoints an executive council, or board, consisting of bishops and other. ministers, to superintend the general affairs of the Brotherhood in the interval between meetings of the General Synod. This council is called the Unity's Elders' Conference. This is divided into three boards—Education, Finance and Missions. The Missions Board has charge of all foreign missions. It names a treasurer, a secretary of missions in England and agents of missions in Germany, England and the United States. Appointments of missionaries and establishment of stations are matters submitted to the whole Unity's Elders' Conference.

The aim of the missionaries is to preach the gospel direct to those to whom they are sent. The awakened are called New People, and are included in the class of catechumens to be instructed. They are not admitted to baptism until their lives show that they really desire to abandon heathenism and become Christians. After baptism they are kept for a while as candidates for the communion. Separate meetings are held for the New People, for those who are to be admitted to baptism, and for candidates for the communion; also for children, single men, single women, married people and widows and widowers.

St. Thomas, in the West Indies, was the first Moravian mission field, and the second was Greenland. While Count Zinzendorf was in Copenhagen he saw two baptized Greenlanders and heard an account of the efforts of Mr. Egede to evangelize that heathen people. There was some thought, he learned, of abandoning the field, the difficulties were so great. He told these things to the Brethren in Herrnhut, as he had those about St. Thomas, and in 1733, five months after the St. Thomas missionaries sailed, a second party started for Greenland and occupied the Southern part as their field, the Danish mission taking the Northern section.

The third mission was to the North American Indians. Other fields entered by the Church, are Guiana, South America, South Africa, among the Hottentots, Kaffirs, and other savages, Barbadoes and other West India islands, Central America, Labrador, Alaska, Central Asia, on the border of Tibet, Australia, among the aborigines, and other countries. Successful missions to lepers are maintained in Jerusalem and in South Africa.

According to latest statistics the Moravians have 137 principal stations, 184 European missionaries, and 33,505 communicants. The receipts in England were in 1898 $68,542; in all the provinces, $125,347.

Organized at Barmen in 1828, this Society is widely known as the Barmen Society. It was formed by the union of small societies at Barmen and Elberfeld, which sent their candidates to Basle seminary to be trained. A training school was opened at Barmen in 1825 and this led to the organization of the Rhenish Mission Society.

South Africa was its first field. There it has three districts: Cape Colony, Namaqua and Herero. The churches in Cape Colony are self-supporting. The communicants include Europeans, imported Negroes, Hottentots, and a mixture of many races. Namaqualand is North of Cape Colony on the West Coast, and Herero is in the center of Damaraland, just North of Namaqualand—both now German territory. The Namaquas, a branch of the Hottentots, are hunters, and a somewhat fierce people. Their country is dry, and unfit for cultivation, and the people are necessarily nomadic in their habits. The Hereros, on the contrary, are a pastoral people. They keep large herds of cattle and are a true Negro tribe. They learn slowly, but hold what they acquire.

The missions in the Dutch East Indies are in Borneo, Sumatra, and Nias. In Borneo and Sumatra the native tribes reached are the Dyaks and the Battas.

The Chinese mission is in the province of Kwantung, among the Puntis.

In 1887 the Society began missionary work in the northern and German portion of New Guinea, among the Papuans.

The Society receives about $120,000 a year. Its list of ordained workers includes 23 missionaries and it has 1,100 native teachers and helpers.

NORTH GERMAN MISSIONARY SOCIETY

This Society was organized in 1836 by missionary unions in Bremen, Hamburg, and other places. Previously these unions had gathered money for other Societies. In those days there was great opposition to missionary societies. Church authorities frowned on such enterprises, the people mocked at them, "no church could be secured for their annual meeting, and notices of them could not be inserted in the papers in connection with religious announcements."

The Society established a missionary institute at Hamburg in 1837, and five years later sent five of its graduates into the field. New Zealand was the first field. The work is no longer among heathen but nominally Christian natives. The African mission is on the Gold Coast. In common with other missions it has suffered from the destructive climate.

The income of the Society, which is supported both by Lutheran and Reformed elements, is about $33,000 a year.

GOSSNER MISSIONARY SOCIETY

This Society is the outcome of the missionary zeal of Pastor Gossner. Gossner was a Roman Catholic, but becoming deeply imbued with evangelical principles he became an evangelical pastor in Berlin. He was one of the directors of the Berlin Missionary Society; but on account of dissatisfaction with the industrial feature of that Society he withdrew from it. Young men came to him to be trained for mission service and went out under the auspices of other societies. In 1842 he was permitted by cabinet ordinance to form a mission society. This Society had no very definite organization, and exercised no control over the missionaries it supported during the lifetime of Gossner. Some of his young men went out on their own account, and by accident, or rather design of Providence, got among the Khols of India, a degraded, stupid people, whom they undertook to evangelize. The field was a desperately hard one, but Gossner gave them no aid except a promise to pray for them. After five long weary years the first baptism took place. Then conversions were rapid. Being under no central authority the missionaries fell out among themselves. Gossner was disturbed, but all he could do was to say, "If you don't agree I shall stop praying for you." The trouble continued for years, and after Gossner's death a split took place and several of the missionaries, with some thousands of converts, went over to the Anglican Society for the Propagation of the Gospel.

The Gossner Society reports over 37,000 adherents in the India field. It received in 1898 upward of $40,000.

LEIPZIG MISSIONARY SOCIETY

This is a Lutheran Missionary Society. It was founded in 1836, with a missionary seminary at Dresden. The aim of the Society is somewhat different from that of Basle, with which it had formerly a connection. As stated from the Leipzig Society's standpoint, the difference is this: the Basle Society aims at individual conversions, and trains its missionaries accordingly; the Leipzig Society seeks national conversion and insists that its missionaries shall have an intimate knowledge of all aspects of civilization—religious, scientific, literary, political and social.

Its mission in India, in Tranquebar, was made over to it by the Danish Mission at Copenhagen. The work is among the Tamils. The Society also has an important mission in Rangoon, Burma. It has in these two countries 36 stations, and upward of 16,000 adherents. Its income is nearly $100,000.

HERMANNSBURG MISSIONARY SOCIETY

Pastor Louis Harms brought about the organization of this Society, in 1849, in Hermannsburg. From the time of his conversion, in 1829, Harms was interested in the mission cause, and in his pastoral relation in Hermannsburg he created such zeal for it that both money and men were offered for the field. The money came from peasants and the candidates were from the farm. Missionary training was provided for them in useful trades as well as in theology. In 1853 eight missionaries were sent out to Africa with the idea that they would support themselves in the field, leaving the Society to bear the expense of sending out. They went to Natal and established an important though difficult mission work among the Zulus. It also has a mission among the Bechuanas, a small undertaking in South India among the Telugus, and stations in Australia and New Zealand.

Since 1877 the Society has served as the organ of the Free Church of Hanover. The secession was due to a new marriage formula issued by the State Church. As it recognized civil marriage Pastor Harms would not use it. Hence the separation. Since 1890 cooperative relations have existed between the Free Church and the State Church, and members of both support the Society.

The annual income is about $58,000 and there are 35,250 adherents in the mission fields.

SCHLESWIG-HOLSTEIN MISSIONARY SOCIETY

This is a Lutheran organization, formed in 1877 for the Lutherans of the province of Schleswig-Holstein. Its headquarters are in Breklum, and it is sometimes, in accordance with German custom, designated as the Breklum Society. It has a mission house and training school in that city. The first missionaries went to the Bastar country, in the central provinces of India. There are now six stations, including the central station in Jeypore.

OTHER GERMAN SOCIETIES

There are several other Societies in Germany, including the Jerusalem Verein, the Berlin Women's Verein, the Neukirchner, the Neuendettelsau, the Evangelical Protestant, and the Evangelical Society, with incomes ranging from less than $4,000 to $15,000 and $20,000.

DANISH MISSION SOCIETY

The Lutheran Church of Denmark was the first of European Churches to attempt foreign mission work among the heathen. As early as 1705 Ziegenbalg and Plütschau, names famous in missionary annals, were ordained in Copenhagen as missionaries, and went out the next year to do work in Tranquebar, India. In 1714 the Royal College of Missions was established in Copenhagen for the training of missionaries. Through this College the State Church maintained missions in India and Greenland. Later on, rationalism came into the Church and the Tamil mission in India passed over to the English. The successor to this movement was the Danish Missionary Society, formed in 1821. It assisted the Greenland mission, but was hampered by the mission college. In 1862 it founded a seminary of its own. Next year a new mission was begun among the Tamils in India. It also has a mission among the Malays in India. The Society represents the State Church.

Besides the Danish Missionary Society, there is in Denmark a small independent society known as Loventhal's, representing the Grundtvigt movement, with a mission in Vellore, India, the Red Karen mission, working among the Karens of Burma, in charge of Schreuder, also of the Grundtvigt movement, and the Northern Santhal Mission, founded by two Danish missionaries, Böresen and Skrefsrud, who left the Gossner mission in India, and began an independent mission among the Santhals, with great success. There is a branch of this mission in a Santhal colony in Assam.

NORWEGIAN MISSION SOCIETY

There was a great evangelical awakening in Norway, in the first quarter of the present century, through the labors of Hans Nilssen Hauge. In consequence of this missionary societies were formed in various places. These societies formed a union in 1843 and the Norwegian Mission Society was the result. It has missions in Zululand and Madagascar. More than 16,000 communicants have been gathered in Madagascar.

This Society represents churches and individuals. Bishop Schreuder, who started the Zulu mission, separated from the Society in 1873, and the Norwegian Church Mission, representing the State Church, was formed to support him. He carried over part of the Zulu mission.

The receipts of the older Society amount to about 350,000 kroners; those of the State Church organization to 7,000 or 8,000 kroners.

SWEDISH MISSIONS

There are four missionary organizations in Sweden: the Swedish Mission Society, Stockholm, organized in 1835, working among the Finns; the Evangelical National Society, Stockholm, organized in 1856, a free movement within the State Church, with missions among the Gallas, in Africa, and the Ghonds in India; the Swedish Church Mission, Stockholm, established in 1874, by authority of the King, for the State Church, with missions among the Zulus of Africa and the Tamils of India; and the Swedish Mission Union, Christinehamn, organized in 1878, to represent the Waldenstromian movement. It is an active society with missions in Russia, Congo, Alaska and North Africa. The North Africa mission is among the Jews of Algiers.

The revenue of the last named Society is about 110,000 kroners, of the Church Mission 46,000 kroners, of the Evangelical Society 137,000 kroners and of the Swedish Society 22,000 kroners.

FINLAND MISSIONARY SOCIETY

This Society was formed in 1857, in connection with the celebration of the seven hundredth anniversary of the Christianization of Finland, by Bishop Henrik, in 1157. A few of the Finnish Lutherans had been stirred by a zeal for missions, but some of the pastors had been haled before the courts for putting up boxes at their doors for missionary contributions. For some years it cooperated with the Gossner Society; but in 1868 it founded a mission of its own in Ovamboland, on the West Coast of South Africa. There are three principal stations.

MISSIONARY SOCIETIES IN HOLLAND

There are six missionary societies in the Netherlands, five representing the Reformed Churches and one the Mennonites.

The Netherlands Missionary Society, Rotterdam, was founded in 1797 through the influence of Dr. Vanderkemp, the South African missionary of the London Society. It has missions in Java, Amboyna and Celebes, with 20,000 communicants. It formerly had missions in India, but they were transferred to English societies.

The Utrecht Society, was organized in 1859. It has work in Dutch New Guinea, or Papua, and in the Moluccas, East Indies.

The Ermelo Society, Ermelo, was founded in

1856, has missions in Talaut Islands, South Seas, in Java and among the Copts in Egypt.

The Dutch Society, Rotterdam, organized in 1858, has work in Western Java and among the Sundaese. The latter are Mohammedans. Many of them have been induced to become Christians.

The Dutch Reformed Society, Rotterdam, was founded in 1859, operates in Central Java, where it has upward of 50 churches, with 5,000 or more communicants.

The Mennonite Society, Amsterdam, has missions in Sumatra and Java.

PARIS EVANGELICAL SOCIETY

This Society was organized in 1822 for missionary work among non-Christian peoples. Jean and Frederick Monod, Baron A. de Staël and Admiral Count Verhnël were among its founders. It is undenominational, but represents, of course, the Reformed faith of France. Its chief mission is among the Basutos of South Africa. The Society also has a mission on the Upper Zambesi River, in the French Colony of Senegambia, on the West Coast, on the Gaboon and Ogove Rivers, and in Tahiti. Its income is upwards of $75,000.

FREE CHURCHES OF SWITZERLAND

The Free Churches of French Switzerland sent missionaries to South Africa in 1874. The mission is in the Transvaal among the Gwamba tribe. The income of the Society is about $15,000.

CHAPTER IX

AMERICAN MISSIONARY SOCIETIES

THE AMERICAN BOARD

DOUBTLESS the attention of the Congregationalists of the United States had been drawn to the subject of missions among the heathen long before the American Board was organized. John Eliot had, in the first half of the seventeenth century, preached to the Indians in their native tongue and soon had a band of "praying Indians." He also trained teachers and preachers for the work. This was the first American mission to the heathen. The formation of the London Missionary Society near the close of the eighteenth century by English Congregationalists was of course known to their American brethren, and helped to crystallize the sentiment which had been forming in favor of the cause.

It was the devotion of young college students which immediately led to the formation of the oldest of the foreign missionary societies of the United States, the American Board of Commissioners for Foreign Missions, at Bradford, Mass., June 29, 1810. The real "birthplace of American Missions" was at Williams college, in the shelter of a haystack, where students held a missionary prayer-meeting in 1806. In this meeting Samuel J. Mills, who had

been consecrated by his mother from his birth
(1783) to missionary service, was a leading spirit.
Two years later, 1808, these godly students formed
in the college a society "to effect, in the person of
its members, a mission to the heathen," but the matter was kept secret lest they "should be thought
rashly imprudent" and should injure the cause they
wished to promote. Mills went to Andover Seminary for his theological education, with Gordon
Hall and James Richards, and there with Samuel
Newell, Adoniram Judson and Samuel Nott, Jr.,
continued to think and pray about the missionary
cause. This led to a request from four of them—
Mills, Newell, Nott and Judson—to the General
Association of Congregational Churches that it
would "attempt a mission to the heathen." Two
others would have joined in this request but for the
fear that so many applicants would alarm the Association. The request was granted without delay,
and the American Board was organized, with nine
commissioners to manage it—five from Massachusetts and four from Connecticut. The Legislature
of Massachusetts refused for two years to grant a
charter, one of the opponents declaring that the
State had no religion to spare for export; but it
was granted June 20, 1812.

The first annual meeting was attended by five
commissioners and an audience of one person. The
receipts for the first year were just 48 cents less than
$1,000. Funds came in so slowly that the London

Missionary Society was asked for help to send out a missionary. It declined, in the hope that resources in the United States would be developed. The same year, 1811, a bequest of $30,000 was received, and it was resolved to send Judson, Nott, Newell and Hall to establish a mission in Asia. They sailed in February, 1812, with Luther Rice; part of the company from New York, part from Philadelphia. The British East India Company would not allow any of them to preach to the Hindus, believing that it would injure their commercial interests. Driven from Calcutta, Judson and Newell went to the Isle of France, Hall and Nott to Bombay, where after a long delay they were given permission to enter upon work and founded the mission among the Marathas. Judson and Rice had changed their views on baptism on the way out, and the former went to Burma and founded the Baptist mission in that country.

In 1811 the Board asked the cooperation of the Presbyterian General Assembly. The response was favorable, and churches of that order contributed to the income of the Board and were represented on the Board of Commissioners. The Associate Reformed Church, the Reformed Dutch and Reformed German Churches also joined the Board. In 1817 the Presbyterian bodies had formed a foreign missionary society for special work among the Indians. In 1825 a union was arranged with the American Board. This continued until the separation of the

Old School and New School parties, the New School Presbyterians supporting the Board until the reunion in 1870. The Reformed Dutch Church withdrew amicably in 1857. Since 1870 the Board has drawn its main support from the Congregational churches, though Presbyterians are still members of it and Presbyterians contribute to it to some extent. Formerly the American Missionary Association, also Congregational, had a few foreign missions, but they were transferred to the Board and it has confined its action to the home field for many years.

The Board is composed of 350 corporate members, at least one third of whom must be laymen and one third ministers. At their annual meeting these corporate members elect the officers of the Board and a Prudential Committee of twelve persons, besides the President and Vice President. The Prudential Committee is charged with the administration of the work and meets twice a month in Boston. There are three Corresponding Secretaries, an Editorial Secretary, a treasurer and a publishing and purchasing agent. There are also two field secretaries.

In 1820, at the end of the first decade of its history, the American Board had missions in West India, Ceylon, among the Cherokee and Choctaw Indians, in the Sandwich Islands, and in Palestine, and the annual income reached nearly $40,000. In the next ten years the Syrian mission and a mission at Canton, China, were started, and the receipts more than doubled. The missions among the Indians, in the Sandwich Islands and in Ceylon were attended with encouraging results and the funds of the Board increased so rapidly that it enlarged its work, began a mission in Constantinople, another in Athens, Greece, and others in Siam, Singapore, Persia, West Africa, and Southeast Africa. At the end of the third decade the Board had 25 missions, 134 ordained missionaries, with physicians, teachers, etc., and 186 female missionaries; making a total force of 365.

At the end of the first fifty years the Board had a large and very successful missionary work under its control. The Sandwich Islands had been virtually Christianized, the missions in India had been strengthened, those in China had been increased, and the beginnings in Africa, Turkey and other countries had been enlarged. The work among the North American Indians had been gradually relinquished to the care of home societies. The receipts of the Board in its fiftieth year were a little less than $430,000.

The sixth decade was made notable by the resignation of Dr. Anderson, who had served as Secretary of the Board for thirty-four years and had conducted its affairs with signal ability and faithfulness, by the beginning of a mission in Japan, and by the withdrawal of the Presbyterian Church from the support of the Board. In 1871 the Sandwich Islands ceased to appear on the list of foreign missions, the work of Christianization having been accomplished, and the Board resolved to undertake work in papal lands. In 1879 the Board, by the will of Asa Otis, received an extraordinary legacy of $1,000,000, which was set apart for new missions, enlargement of existing missions, and educational purposes. The income of the Board in 1898 was $687,200, including the contributions of its missions, amounting to $116,753. In that year it had 101 principal stations, 1,271 out-stations, 539 missionaries, 2,975 native laborers, 465 churches and 47,023 communicants.

The missions of the Board, twenty in number, are in Asia, Africa, Europe, Mexico and the Pacific islands. Its extensive missions among the American Indians were transferred some years ago to home organizations. The Arcot mission in India and the Amoy mission in China were transferred to the Reformed Dutch Church when the latter organized its own foreign board. The Persian, Syrian and Gaboon missions went to the Presbyterian Board, as its share of the work, on the reunion in 1870.

The oldest of the missions are the Marathi and the Ceylon. Of the missionaries first sent out Mr. and Mrs. Judson went to Burma as Baptists, Luther Rice returned to America to raise support for them. There remained, of the original company, Messrs. Nott, Hall and Newell. Driven from Calcutta,

Messrs. Nott and Hall went to Bombay. They were allowed to stay, and laid the foundations of the Marathi mission. Mr. Newell went to Mauritius, losing his wife and child on the way. He sailed thence in a Portuguese ship and touched at Ceylon. Finding Ceylon open, and believing the brethren at Bombay would have to leave there, he began missionary work among the Ceylonese. The Marathi mission, begun under discouraging circumstances, has grown steadily in prosperity and influence among a population of 3,000,000. The Ceylon mission includes a number of self-supporting churches and has a native foreign missionary society. The third mission in India is the Madura, begun in 1834, among about 2,000,000 Tamils. The natives treated the missionaries contemptuously at first, as outcasts of the white race, later with active enmity. But Christianity has made its way and has slowly undermined the heathen system.

The beginning of the mission in the Sandwich Islands was clearly providential. October 23, 1819, seventeen persons, two of them ordained, sailed from Boston in the brig *Thaddeus* for the islands. The number embraced three native Hawaiians who had been driven from the islands by civil war and had been educated in the missionary school established by the Board in New Haven, Conn. It was a very serious undertaking at that time; not simply because the passage was so long and tedious but because the Hawaiians were understood to be fierce and warlike heathen. When the expedition reached the group, however, it was found that the people had abolished idolatry and were ready for Christianity. The king, with twelve chiefs and 200 pupils, went to school to the missionaries, and so anxious were the people to learn that eleven years after the first expedition sailed from Boston there were 900 schools in the islands, with 44,000 learners. Christianity speedily uprooted and replaced heathenism, and converts went out from Hawaii to Christianize the Marquesas Islands, under the auspices of the Hawaiian Missionary Society, which was organized in 1850. The Micronesian missions, in the Gilbert, Marshall and Caroline Islands, begun in 1851, have been very successful.

The Board's missions among populations belonging to the Oriental Christian Churches were begun by Pliny Fisk and Levi Parsons in 1821. The outcome is an extensive work among the Armenians of Turkey, divided into the Western, Central and Eastern Turkey missions. In connection with these missions the Greek and Hebrew populations are also reached to some extent. The Moslems are only affected indirectly, as work among them is not tolerated. The Armenians have been extensively evangelized, and many churches with native pastors are to be found in European and Asiatic Turkey. The terrible massacre of Armenians by the Turks a few years ago will long be remembered for its fiendishness, for the number of the victims, and for the sublime courage with which men and women met death; preferring the sword to apostasy to the Moslem faith. The world has hardly ceased to ring with the cries of horror and indignation with which civilized nations received the reports of the awful acts of the bloody Turk. The mission in Bulgaria, south of the Balkans, has achieved important results for this vigorous race. Many of its young men have been educated at Robert College, in Constantinople, which has been a center of strong religious influence.

The Board's oldest mission in China, the Amoy, went to the Board of the Reformed Dutch Church. The next oldest mission, the Foochow, begun in 1847, is not so strong as the North China. Both are flourishing missions. There is also a considerable work in the province of Shansi and a mission in Hongkong.

The African missions operated by the Board are among the Zulus in Natal, and the Transvaal, in East Central Africa, and in West Central Africa. The latter, with its chief stations at Bailundu and Chisamba in Benguela, was established in 1880. The missionaries were expelled in 1883, but returned in 1885 and resumed their work. The three African missions have sixteen stations, 57 American laborers.

The Board has a strong mission in Japan, begun in 1869. There are 72 churches, and over ten thousand communicants. The Doshisha, or Training

School at Kioto, under native control was carried astray and the Board ceased to be responsible for it; but in 1899 it was returned to the Board and is again a definitely Christian school.

Missions in papal lands were begun in 1872. They are in Mexico, Spain and Austria, all established in the same year. There are 17 churches in Mexico, 16 in Austria, and 8 in Spain. In Austria the work is among the Bohemians and is prosperous.

The Board has in all 101 stations, 1,271 out-stations, 465 churches, 47,023 communicants, with 1,270 schools and 56,641 under instruction. The number of American laborers is 539, and of native laborers 2,975, of whom 477 are preachers.

AMERICAN BAPTIST MISSIONARY UNION

The immediate occasion of the organization of this Society, May 18, 1814, four years after the American Board had come into existence, was the news sent back to American Baptists that Adoniram Judson and Luther Rice, missionaries to India of the American Board, had changed their views on the way out as to the proper subjects and method of baptism, and become Baptists. In expectation of meeting missionaries of the English Baptist Society at Calcutta they had studied the New Testament to prepare to defend the Congregational teaching, but had become convinced that the Baptists were right and they themselves wrong, and instead of engaging in controversy with the Baptist missionaries they sought baptism at their hands. Letters announcing their change of belief were sent to America, and Baptists were asked to support them. Luther Rice returned to the United States to promote this object, and found on his arrival that an organization with this end in view had already been formed.

The Baptists had previously had their attention drawn to the missionary cause, and had been contributing to the English Baptist Missionary Society which had sent Carey to India in 1793. The Rev. William Stoughton, who had been present at the organization of the English Society at Kettering, had emigrated to America the next year and communicated some of his missionary enthusiasm to American Baptists. English missionaries, who touched at New York or Boston on their way to India, also awakened zeal for this cause. Besides, letters came frequently from Carey and his colaborers in India, and were published in a magazine established by a Baptist home missionary society in Massachusetts. The result was the formation of societies in Boston, New York, Philadelphia and other cities for the prosecution of the mission begun under such peculiar circumstances. These societies were united in the "General Convention" of the Baptists of the United States "for Foreign Missions," organized at a meeting in Philadelphia, May 18, 1814. The first Corresponding Secretary of the Society was the Rev. William Stoughton, who had heard Carey's famous sermon, "Expect great things from God, attempt great things for God." He served until 1826, when the headquarters of the Society were removed from Philadelphia to Boston.

When the American Baptists entered upon foreign mission work they numbered about 70,000 only. They were widely scattered along the Atlantic coast, with no general bond of union. The centers were in Massachusetts and Rhode Island, in Philadelphia and Virginia. The missionary Convention, which was held triennially, drew Baptists together from all parts of the country and led to the founding of other important denominational enterprises. In 1817 it authorized the use of a portion of the funds for home missions, and later on the Publication Society was organized. The slavery question, which divided so many denominations, brought about a separation of the Northern and Southern Baptists in 1846, when the triennial Convention was discontinued and the American Baptist Missionary Union was formed to represent Northern and the Southern Board to represent Southern Baptists in foreign work. The separation did not long or severely affect the receipts of the Union. In 1851 they reached $118,726, the highest point during its history. The average had been about $75,000. Since the Civil War they have risen steadily. In 1864 the amount received was $135,012; in 1874 $261,581; and in the centenary year, 1893, the income was $766,783. With the contributions in the mission fields the average yearly income is more than $700,000.

The annual meeting of the Union is held in May in connection with the anniversaries of other denominational societies. It consists of missionaries, life and honorary members, and delegates from churches and associations. It elects the board of managers of the Union, consisting of seventy-five members, of whom not more than two-fifths shall be ministers. This board elects an Executive Committee of fifteen, as nearly equally divided as possible between the lay and clerical elements. The Executive Committee is charged with the direct administration of the affairs of the Union. It meets twice a month, the members giving their services. There are two corresponding secretaries, one in charge of the missions abroad, the other of the work at home, including the direction of the district secretaries, correspondence with applicants for appointment as missionaries, etc.

The fields of the Union are in Asia, Africa and Europe. When Judson was driven out of India the only vessel on which he could secure passage for himself and wife was bound to Rangoon. There was begun the first Baptist mission among the Burmese. It was gradually extended to the Sgau Karen, Pwo Karen, Shan, Kachin and Chin races. Judson soon learned the language well enough to read and talk in it, and began almost immediately the preparation of a Burmese grammar and dictionary and the translation of portions of the Bible. In 1819 he began to preach to the people in their own tongue, and the next year baptized the first Burman convert to Christianity. The work in Rangoon was greatly disturbed by opposition of Buddhist rulers, and suspended during several considerable periods, until that part of Burma became, in 1852, British territory. During the enforced absence of the American missionaries the Burman church was maintained by a native pastor and only one of the members fell away. Work among the Karens, who are the peasant population, was begun by George Dana Boardman and his wife in 1828. Although it was attended by much persecution it steadily developed until there were nearly 500 Karen churches in all Burma. Ko-thah-byu, a slave converted under the labors of Judson and baptized by Boardman, was the first Karen convert and the first Karen preacher. He was so zealous and successful as an evangelist that he has been called the "Karen Apostle."

Assam, which is northwest of Burma, was entered in 1836, by Burman missionaries. The work was at first among the Assamese, Shans and Khamtis, and grammars, dictionaries, etc., were prepared, and the Scriptures translated into these tongues. Subsequently many of the hill tribes were reached and now the most flourishing of the three missions is that among the Garos.

Arakan, which lies on the Bay of Bengal, became a mission field of the Union in 1835. The natives are of Burman stock. In the Northern part the climate was singularly fatal to missionaries and finally the field was abandoned. So was the Southern mission for a different reason. After 35 years it was occupied again in 1888.

The Siam mission was established in 1833 by John Taylor Jones, who went to Bangkok, the capital, from Maulmain, Burma. Two years later a mission to the Chinese in Bangkok was undertaken by William Dean. The work among the Siamese has not been very successful, but that among the Chinese was regarded as an important door into China.

In addition to Chinese work in Bangkok mission stations were opened at Hongkong, at Macao and at Swatow in 1861. Besides the South China and Central China missions, the Union has missions in East China, with headquarters at Ningpo, and in West China, at Suchau.

In Southern India, a mission among the Telugus, on the Bay of Bengal, was begun at Nellore in 1836. This was a hard and stubborn field, and there were twenty years of dreary waiting for the first native convert. After thirty years of patient endeavor there were not above twenty-four Telugu converts. Several times the Union had discussed the question of abandoning a field which offered no inducements for the continued outlay of money; but Dr. Jewett resolutely refused to abandon the field. In 1865 the Union sent the Rev. J. E. Clough to reinforce the "lone star mission," as it was called; for while the stars indicating Baptist missions had multiplied in Burma, across the bay to the westward the Telugu country had only one star for a generation.

Clough began work in Ongole, north of Nellore. Almost immediately prosperity began at both stations, chiefly at the new one. After nine years there were 336 members at Nellore, 2,761 at Ongole, 675 at Ramapatam, and 60 at Allur. Then came severe famine; after the famine, flood, cholera, and then a severer famine. Many of the converts died; but the missionaries labored to save the people; administering the relief which came from the government and from charity so wisely as to win the gratitude of the surviving heathen. After the famine they pressed by hundreds and thousands for admission to the Church, and after careful examination 8,691 were baptized within a period of six weeks in 1878; 2,222 in one day. The work continued and the "lone star mission" became the most prosperous mission of the Union, with at least 100,000 adherents. The Sudras, laboring caste, merchants, and the military caste, also many Brahmins, surrendered caste and became active Christians. A large proportion of the churches are self-supporting.

The Japanese mission was undertaken in 1872, where there is a large force of American missionaries and a theological seminary for the training of native pastors.

The first work by Baptist missionaries in Africa was among the American colonists on the Liberian coast. A mission to the native Bassas was begun but was abandoned, in 1856, on account of fatalities among the missionaries. Desiring to have a mission among the heathen the Union gladly received the work of the Livingstone Inland Mission, offered, in 1883, by Mr. and Mrs. H. Grattan Guinness, its founders. The Guinnesses, who were English people, began the mission in the Congo Free State and established six stations, with twenty-five missionaries. The Union took the missions under its charge in 1884, and has since extended them to the Upper Congo, where a steamer plies between the stations.

The European missions of the Union are in both Protestant and Catholic countries. The French work was begun in 1832. For many years native pastors were persecuted, and up to 1876 missionary work in the provinces was punished by fines and confiscations. The mission is affiliated with the McAll movement. The mission in Germany was begun in 1834, when Dr. Barnas Sears baptized seven persons in the River Elbe. One of these converts, Johann Gerhard Oncken, became the first pastor of the first Baptist church, and visited many cities as a missionary. The work spread rapidly and although it was attended with persecution it was prosperous. It was extended to Denmark, Hungary, Austria, Switzerland, and other countries, all by German missionaries. The entire work in Protestant Europe has been prosecuted by natives, no missionaries having been sent out by the Union from this country. There are Baptist churches in St. Petersburg, in Southern Russia, also in Bulgaria, Roumania, Bosnia and the Caucasus.

Norwegians and Swedes who were sailors on the ship that carried Baptist missionaries to Burma, and who had been converted by their labors, began missionary work in Sweden in 1817. Swedes converted in New York City went back to their country in 1834-5, and in 1848 the first Swedish Baptist church was organized at Gothenburg. The work spread gradually until a score of Baptist associations were created. Most of the churches are self-supporting.

The mission in Spain, begun in Madrid in 1868 and adopted by the Union in 1870, has prospered, despite much persecution, and there are churches in many provinces.

The only work carried on in America by the Union was among the Indians, begun in 1817. In 1865 the last of these was transferred to the American Baptist Home Missionary Society.

MISSIONARY SOCIETY OF THE METHODIST EPISCOPAL CHURCH

To the early Methodists the United States was itself missionary ground, and Boardman, Pilmoor, Asbury and others sent over from England were missionaries. Dr. Thomas Coke, as early as 1786, after his visit to this country in connection with the organization of the Methodist Episcopal Church, established missions in the West Indies. In 1814 he sailed from England with a company of missionaries for India, but was not permitted to see that country, as he died on the way and was buried at sea.

The early Methodist preachers in this country, absorbed as they were in the growing work here, were not drawn toward foreign fields as early as their British brethren and their brethren of other denominations in the United States. There were some who favored the organization of a missionary society, but only for work in this country. It was a revival among the Wyandot Indians under the preaching of John Stewart, a colored man just recovered from a sinful life and intemperate habits, which led to the formation of the Missionary Society in New York City April 5, 1819. There was some doubt whether such a society was necessary, and there was opposition to it on various grounds for some years. One objection was that it was organized as a Bible Society as well as a Missionary Society, and the friends of the American Bible Society thought that Methodists should have their Bible work done through that organization. This view prevailed after a time, and the Society became strictly a missionary organization. The General Conference of 1820 heartily approved of the new society and said that the missionary spirit was the life blood of Methodism; and that, while the time might not yet have come to send missionaries beyond the seas, there were large fields in this country, particularly among the Indians, which should be entered.

The receipts of the first year were $823.04, and those of the second year $2,329. At the end of the first decade they exceeded $14,000. They increased rapidly and in 1838 were over $96,000. In 1839 they were $132,480, and in 1844, $146,579. The separation of the Southern Conferences in that year reduced the income, but in 1852 the loss had been more than regained, the receipts being $151,982. The next year the income leaped to $338,068, but fell off to less than $300,000 for the next nine years. They passed the half million line in 1864, and the million line in 1886. The receipts for 1899 were $1,376,399, the largest in the history of the Society.

The missionary interests of the Church are committed by the General Conference to two bodies. First, the General Missionary Committee, consisting of the Bishops, the Secretaries and Treasurers of the Society, fourteen representatives of General Conference districts, and fourteen representatives, half clerical and half lay, of the Board of Managers. This General Committee has the power to establish or discontinue missions and to make annual appropriations. Second, the Board of Managers, consisting of the Bishops, thirty-two laymen and thirty-two ministers, who are appointed by the General

Conference. This Board is charged with the duties of administration. There are three Corresponding Secretaries, a Recording Secretary, a Treasurer and an Assistant Treasurer.

The first missionary of the Society was sent to the French in New Orleans. Stewart's work among the Indians was strengthened. Missions to the English speaking population were begun, particular attention being given to the colored people; and from time to time various classes of immigrants from foreign countries have been taken within the scope of the Society's labors.

The foreign work of the Society was begun in 1832, when Melville B. Cox was sent to Africa to labor among the persons colonized in Liberia by the American Colonization Society. He sailed from Norfolk, Va., November 6, 1832, and arrived at Monrovia March 7, 1833. He did not expect to live long in Africa, saying before he sailed, "If God please that my bones shall lie in an African grave, I shall have established such a bond between Africa and the Church at home as shall not be broken till Africa be redeemed." His apprehensions proved to be well founded. He caught the fever, and in four and a half months was laid in an African grave. His epitaph, given before he left the United States, was, "Let a thousand fall before Africa be given up!" These words have prevented the interest of the Church in the Dark Continent from dying out, although the outlook has at times been dark.

Two Missionary Bishops, Burns and Roberts, both colored men, were successively chosen for the African Mission. After the death of Roberts no other Bishop was chosen for that field until 1884, when William Taylor was elected and consecrated Missionary Bishop of Africa. For twelve years he performed much zealous labor in establishing a number of missions on the border of Liberia and on the Congo in Angola, on the self-supporting plan. He was retired in 1896 and Joseph C. Hartzell was elected as his successor. Bishop Hartzell has organized and strengthened the whole work and added new stations. There are now two Annual Conferences—the Liberia Conference and the Congo Mission Conference. The latter includes not only the river territory and a considerable work in Angola, but also a district in Southeastern Africa, with headquarters at Inhambane on the coast, and a district in Mashonaland north of Matabeleland and west of the Portuguese territory, through which the Zambesi river runs. Much attention is given to industrial work as well as to evangelistic and school work, and great hopes are entertained of future success in all parts of the mission.

The second foreign mission was established in South America in 1835 by Fountain E. Pitts. It was begun in the city of Buenos Ayres, where work has been done in both English and Spanish and from which center openings in other countries have been made from time to time, until Uruguay and Paraguay have been opened and a little work has also been done in South Brazil. Among the early laborers were Rev. Justin Spaulding and Rev. John Dempster. Rev. Daniel P. Kidder was also among the effective laborers in Brazil. The work in Brazil was given up in 1841, and nothing further was done in that country until Rev. Justus H. Nelson and wife went to Para, in 1880, with Rev. William Taylor, since which time the work has been continued.

Dr. Dallas D. Lore was among the early missionaries in Buenos Ayres. Rev. Goldsmith D. Carrow succeeded Dr. Lore, and was followed in 1856 by Rev. William Goodfellow, who was the efficient superintendent for thirteen years. During the week of prayer in 1860 John F. Thomson was converted at Buenos Ayres and has since been one of the most faithful missionaries in the work. Rev. Henry G. Jackson, D.D., served for ten years, from 1868 to 1878. Rev. Thomas B. Wood was in charge for a time, and was succeeded in 1886 by Rev. Charles W. Drees, formerly of the Mexico Mission, who has been at his post until this year (1900), when he was appointed to open work in Puerto Rico.

Mr. Wood began work in Rosario in 1870, and Mr. Thomson in Montevideo in 1868, since which time the work in Uruguay has gone on successfully.

In 1887 William Taylor sailed from New York for the West Coast of South America, visited many places in Peru and Chili, and established work at a number of stations, his purpose being to make the work self-supporting and to secure money for carrying on evangelistic work from the proceeds of schools. A Transit and Building Fund was organized to aid him in carrying on his work, of which Mr. Anderson Fowler and Mr. Richard Grant were leading supporters. In 1893 that Society offered to convey to the Missionary Society all their missions and property in Chili on condition that the Society would conduct the work in that country on the self-supporting plan. The General Committee accepted the offer and recommended the Board of Managers to receive and administer the missions, which was done in 1894, but the action was subsequently to some extent reconsidered and, after some changes, in 1897 an agreement was reached by which the Missionary Society was to retain the missions and the property and conduct them on the self-supporting plan, from which it would not depart except in case of extreme necessity.

The work in Peru, which has been under the charge of Dr. Thomas B. Wood since 1891, has met with much trouble, but has a successful footing in that land.

The Woman's Foreign Missionary Society has had excellent workers both on the East and West Coast, Miss Jennie M. Chapin and Miss L. B. Denning being sent to Rosario in 1874, and other excellent ladies following at various times since.

The work on the East Coast constitutes the South America Conference, while that in Peru and Chili is organized into the Western South America Mission Conference.

China was designated as a mission field by the General Missionary Committee in May, 1846. The first missionaries sent out were Judson Dwight Collins and Moses C. White, who sailed from Boston April 15, 1847, and reached Foochow September 6. They were followed by Rev. Henry Hickok and Rev. Robert S. Maclay, who arrived April 15, 1848. In 1851 Rev. I. W. Wiley, afterward Bishop, with his wife, the Rev. James Colder and wife and Miss M. Seely were added to the mission. Dr. Erastus Wentworth and Rev. Otis Gibson and their wives arrived in 1855, and Dr. S. L. Baldwin and wife, with the Misses Beulah and Sarah H. Woolston and Miss Phebe E. Potter, in 1859, since which time numbers of missionaries have been added, a few have died, and some have from time to time retired—from the work. Much attention has been given to the evangelistic work, and no mission in China has been more successful in winning converts and organizing them into churches than the mission at Foochow. The first converts were received in 1857. In 1862 the number of members was 87.

The mission sent out in 1867 the first missionaries to Central China, Rev. V. C. Hart and Rev. E. S. Todd, who began work at Kiukiang, which work has now grown into the large and successful Central China Mission. In 1869 it also sent Rev. L. N. Wheeler and Rev. H. H. Lowry to Peking, who laid the foundations of the work of the North China Mission.

The Foochow Conference was organized by Bishop Wiley December 6, 1867, by which time the number of members and probationers had reached 2,011. The native preachers who were appointed presiding elders on the organization of this Conference, namely, Hu Po Mi, Hu Yong Mi, Sia Sek Ong, Yek Ing Kwang, and Li Yu Mi, had been raised up in the mission; all having been converted as adults except Yek Ing Kwang, who was converted while a student in the boys' boarding school. The mission has continued to grow and prosper up to this date.

In 1896 the work in the Hing Hua prefecture and surrounding regions had grown to such an extent that a Mission Conference was organized and is making very rapid progress towards self-support. The North China Mission was organized as a Conference in 1894.

The West China Mission in Sz-Chuen province was ordered by the General Missionary Committee in November, 1880, and Dr. L. N. Wheeler, formerly of the Foochow and North China Missions, with his family, and Rev. Spencer Lewis and wife, sailed from San Francisco September 6, 1881, and arrived at Chung King December 3. The mission, although broken up by riot in 1885 and suffering much tribulation at various times since that date, has been successful and is now well established.

The Woman's Foreign Missionary Society has done most valuable work in China, and its pioneers, the Misses Woolston, Dr. Sigourney Trask, Miss Clara Cushman, Miss Gertrude Howe, Miss Lucy H. Hoag, M.D., and their successors, are held in grateful remembrance. The following table, compiled from the latest reports at hand, will show the present statistics of the missions in China in some important particulars:

	Members.	Probationers.	Total.	Benevolent Contribut'ns.	Self-support.
Foochow.............	4,349	4,301	8,650	$777	$3,488
Hinghua.............	2,338	2,949	5,287	1,885	4,156
Central China........	1,531	2,478	4,009	141	5,453
North China.........	3,738	2,904	6,642	529	3,563
West China.........	219	118	337	31	172
Total............	12,175	12,750	24,925	$3,363	$17,832

The mission to Japan was inaugurated in 1872; Dr. R. S. Maclay, who had been superintendent of the Foochow Mission for a quarter of a century, being appointed to open the work there. He arrived with his family in Yokohama June 11, 1873. Rev. J. C. Davison, Rev. Julius Soper and Rev. M. C. Harris were appointed at the outset. The

Rev. I. H. Correll, who was originally appointed to Foochow but detained at Yokohama on account of the serious illness of his wife during the voyage, was also transferred to the Japan mission. The formal organization of the mission took place August 8, 1873, in Yokohama, under the presidency of Bishop Harris. It was decided to occupy at once stations in different portions of the empire, Hakodate being chosen for the North, Yokohama and Tokyo for the Center, and Nagasaki for the South. Other missionaries have been added, the evangelistic and educational work has been carried on with much energy, and although the work has been subject to many vicissitudes it has made noticeable progress. The Japan Conference was organized by Bishop Wiley at Yokohama August 15, 1884, the number of members at that time being 907 and probationers 241. In 1898 the South Japan Conference was organized, at which time there were in the whole empire over 5,000 communicants connected with the Church. The Woman's Foreign Missionary Society has nobly sustained its work in the empire since its first missionary, Miss Dora E. Schoonmaker, was sent out, in 1874. The names of such ladies as Miss Elizabeth Russell, Miss M. A. Spencer, Miss Minnie S. Hampton, and many others, are well known in the Christian world, and are a sufficient guarantee for faithful and successful work.

Korea, so long known as "the hermit nation,"

had been open to foreign commerce and settlement but a short time when this Society entered upon work in that land. Dr. R. S. Maclay had pioneered the work by visiting the country and making a report on it to the Board at home. Dr. W. B. Scranton and Rev. H. G. Appenzeller were appointed to open the mission and the work was begun, in 1885, at Seoul, the capital. In after years stations were opened at Chemulpo, Pyeng Yang and Wonsan, and the work has been increasing in interest and importance. Mrs. M. F. Scranton, the mother of Dr. W. B. Scranton, was the pioneer of the Woman's Foreign Missionary Society, and has been aided by a noble band of sisters who have since gone to the field. More than two thousand communicants are now connected with the mission and the opportunities for successful work seem to be among the best in the whole foreign field.

. The work in India was begun in 1856 by the Rev. William Butler. After looking over the ground he chose the valley of the Ganges, in Northwest India, as the field of operations. Assisted by Joel T. Janvier, a native interpreter given him by the American Presbyterian Mission at Allahabad, he began work in Bareilly. The next year the great Sepoy rebellion began. Dr. Butler and family, by a timely removal to Naini Tal, fortunately escaped the mutineers, who were putting all foreigners to death. The journey to that place in the Himalayas was attended with great suffering from hunger, exposure and the hardships of travel, and was not without danger from wild beasts and assassins. Bareilly was re-occupied in 1859. Meantime much had been done at Naini Tal and other convenient points. From these beginnings amid the trials and tribulations of a great uprising and massacre wonderful developments have followed. The work has spread all over India, across the border on the east into Burma, and on the southeast into Malaysia. In that territory there are now five Annual Conferences and one Mission Conference, and the total number of communicants is about 80,000. From the Malaysia Conference equipment for a mission in the Philippines has been obtained, under the superintendence of Bishop Thoburn.

Among the early associates of Dr. Butler were Rev. Messrs. J. L. Humphrey, E. W. Parker, C. W. Judd, J. R. Downey and J. M. Thoburn. The work has been strongly reinforced in later years as occasion has demanded.

The work of William Taylor in South India in 1870 and following years led to the organization of English-speaking congregations in that part of the country and also to work among the natives. It was at first independent of the Missionary Society, but was connected with the India Conference, in 1874, under the name of the Bombay and Bengal Mission, of which William Taylor was made superintendent. Bishop Harris, arriving in Calcutta in

December, 1873, transferred Rev. J. M. Thoburn from North India to Calcutta, to take the place of William Taylor, who wished to be relieved for further evangelistic work. Since that date the work has continued to grow in all directions. Dr. Thoburn was elected Missionary Bishop of India and Malaysia by the General Conference of 1884.

While there has been considerable progress in other portions of the work, the greatest successes of the mission have been attained in the old North India region, which is now divided into the North India and Northwest India Conferences, and where there are now over 70,000 communicants, with a much larger demand for preaching and the presence of teacher-pastors than the mission is able to meet. The work of the Woman's Foreign Missionary Society has been very successful in this great field; from the time that Miss Isabella Thoburn and Dr. Clara A. Swain were sent out a number of most excellent ladies have been sent to the field and their work has been crowned with great success. In the three branches, school work, evangelistic work, and medical work, it has been among the most notable agencies in promoting the spirit of Christianity in India.

The work of the Society in Mexico was inaugurated by Dr. William Butler, founder of the mission in India, in 1873, when the Empire of Maximilian had but recently been overthrown and Jesuits and other Roman Catholic orders had been expelled by the Juarez government. The ancient palace of Montezuma, in the City of Mexico, which had been occupied as a monastery for three centuries, was purchased to serve as headquarters of the Methodist Mission. Rev. Thomas Carter, D.D., arrived in Mexico March 13, 1873, and was followed by C. W. Drees and J. W. Butler, son of the superintendent, May 9, 1874. Property was purchased and work commenced in Puebla, and afterwards in Miraflores, Orizaba, Guanajuato, and other centers. An Annual Conference was organized by Bishop W. L. Harris in Trinity Church, Mexico City, January 15, 1885. At that time there were 674 probationers and 625 full members. There are now over 5,000 communicants. The mission has not been without severe persecution in some portions of the work at times, but has steadily grown, and the right to religious freedom has been strongly upheld by President Diaz wherever occasion demands. The Woman's Foreign Missionary Society has been an efficient helper in this as in other fields. Miss S. M. Warner and Miss Mary Hastings, the pioneers, went out in 1874, and have been followed by a noble band, prominent among whom in later years have been Miss Mary De F. Loyd, Miss Amelia Van Dorsten, Miss Harriet Ayres, and other efficient workers.

There are nine other foreign missions of the Methodist Episcopal Church, all in Europe. The prosperous work in Germany is due largely to the interest in the Germans caused by the conversion of William Nast and others in this country. He visited Germany in 1844, by appointment, and on his return it was determined to establish a mission there. It succeeded, and the work spread to Switzerland. In these two countries there are three Conferences, with more than 18,000 members. Scandinavians who had been converted in this country, many of them in the Bethel ship "John Wesley" in the harbor of New York, carried the gospel back to Norway, where O. P. Peterson, who went out in 1849, had conducted successful revival meetings for nearly a year. He was appointed a missionary in 1853. From this have sprung the prosperous missions of Norway, Sweden and Denmark. An important work was begun in Finland in 1884, connected with which is also one church in St. Petersburg. Bulgaria was entered in 1857. This field has been a very difficult one and results have not been as encouraging as in the other missions of the Society. It embraces that part of the principality lying north of the Balkans. The number of communicants is less than 250. The question of a mission to Italy was agitated more than forty years before the mission was actually begun. Dr. Leroy M. Vernon began the work in 1871. A church was opened in 1873 in Bologna, and Florence was occupied in the same year, after which Milan and Perugia were entered and work was taken up in Rome in 1875. The Annual Conference was organized in 1880. Dr. William Burt was sent out in 1885, and on Dr. Vernon's retirement from the mission in 1888, after seventeen years of faithful service, Dr. Burt was put in charge. This mission has had a less number of foreign laborers than any other foreign mission, and has at present but three on the field. The Woman's Foreign Missionary Society has done efficient school work under the direction of Miss Emma H. Hall and Miss Ella Vickery. Some men of distinction have been received into the mission from the Roman Catholic Church, and its work seems to have been of sufficient importance to attract the attention of the Pope, who has recently manifested his opposition to it and sanctioned with his blessing a society whose express purpose is to antagonize its work. There are at present over 2,000 communicants in this mission.

The Society supports in all its foreign fields 28 missions, which report an aggregate of more than 180,000 communicants. There are over 1,000 churches and chapels, valued at two and three fourths million dollars; 16 theological schools, with 314 students; 58 high schools with 4,622 pupils, and 32,000 pupils in day schools. There are 4,300 Sunday schools, with 187,000 pupils.

REFORMED (DUTCH) BOARD OF MISSIONS

The Reformed Church was introduced into America with the first Dutch settlers in New York, early in the seventeenth century, and in 1643 began to labor among the Mohawks. The sturdy Hollanders were among the first to catch the missionary spirit and become interested in what was done in England for missions at the close of the eighteenth century. In 1796 they united with Baptists and Presbyterians in organizing the New York Missionary Society "for the purpose of offering their prayers to the God of grace, that he would be pleased to pour out his Spirit on his Church and send his Gospel to all nations." The Society, however, did not contemplate foreign missions, but hoped to do something for the Indians. This was similar to other local societies which sprang up in various centers of population. In response to an invitation from the Presbyterian General Assembly in 1816 the Reformed General Synod appointed commissioners to arrange a plan for the formation of a Society for Foreign Missions. The result was the United Missionary Society, formed the same year, for missionary work among the Indians in Mexico and South America and in other portions of the heathen world. In it were associated the Presbyterian, Associate Reformed and Dutch Reformed Churches. The missions and property of the New York Missionary Society were conveyed to the new organization in 1821, and in 1826 the United Society was incorporated with the American Board.

In 1832 the Dutch Church resolved to have a Board of Foreign Missions of its own but carry on the work through the American Board. This coöperation continued until 1857, when a separation was arranged by which the Arcot mission in India and the Amoy mission in China were ceded by the American Board to the Dutch Board. During this period the latter had its own treasury and appropriated its money to the support of missionaries selected from its own Church, or to special objects, the American Board accepting the missionaries so designated and conducting the missions. A number of missionaries were designated for a new mission in Borneo, begun in 1836 but discontinued in 1849, and some of the missionaries went to Amoy.

In 1850 a work among the Tamils in India was undertaken. The Rev. John Scudder, M.D., who had been laboring in Ceylon since 1819, removed to Madras in 1836 and labored in connection with that mission. In 1846 he was joined by his eldest son, Henry Martyn Scudder. The latter settled at Arcot in 1850, and was joined in 1852 by his brothers William and Joseph. This was the foundation of the present flourishing Arcot mission.

The Church believed that it could best develop its missionary spirit and resources by independent organization, and accordingly separation took place in 1857. In that year the Church's income amounted to $12,304; the next year it doubled. In the first ten years after separation the receipts reached a total of $469,067; nearly twice as much as had been raised in the previous quarter of a century. Including contributions on the mission field the Board now raises about $125,000 a year.

The Board consists of twenty-four members. chosen by the General Synod for the term of three years, one third of the number changing every year. Half of the members must be ministers. The Board meets once a quarter. The immediate oversight of the business of the Board is committed to an Executive Committee, of five ministers and five laymen, elected annually by the Board. The schedule of appropriations is prepared by the Finance Committee of three chosen by the Executive Committee, from estimates received from the missions, and is approved by the Board. One corresponding secretary is employed.

The missions of the Board are in India, China, Japan, and among Arabic-speaking Moslems and slaves.

The Arcot mission in India has already been mentioned. The Amoy mission in China is among a population of about 3,000,000. That of Japan, belonging to the "United Church of Christ in Japan," has three stations. It was established in 1859. The Arabian mission, begun independently by Prof. J. G. Lansing and three others in 1889, was received under the care of the Board in 1894.

In all, the Board has 22 stations, 89 American missionaries, 282 native laborers, 47 churches and 5,564 communicants.

REFORMED (GERMAN) BOARD

The Board of Foreign Missions of the Reformed Church in the United States was the outcome of a suggestion of the Board of Home Missions, and was organized in 1838, at Lancaster, Penn. From 1840 to 1865 it contributed to the support of the Rev. Benjamin Schneider, D.D., laboring under the auspices of the American Board. At the latter date, the Church decided to withdraw its support from the American Board and to have missions of its own. Until its mission in Japan was established it divided its funds between the Winnebago Indians and a mission in India. Since the opening of the Japan mission, following on the reorganization of the Board in 1873, that has been its only foreign mission. There are two stations, 56 out-stations, 16 American and 37 native laborers, 8 churches, and 1,950 communicants.

The Board consists of twelve members—8 clerical and 4 lay—elected by the General Synod. The officers and an additional member chosen by the Board constitute the Executive Committee, charged with administrative oversight.

The annual income is about $28,000.

PRESBYTERIAN BOARD

The earliest mission work done by the Presbyterian Church as a denomination among the Indians was through a Scottish Society for the "Propagation of Christian Knowledge," and the beginning-ning was in 1741. Azariah Horton and David Brainerd, names not destined soon to be forgotten, were the first missionaries. Those who succeeded them were supported almost entirely by funds raised by American Presbyterian churches which took a lively interest in the work. After the Revolutionary War these missions were almost abandoned until 1796, when they were renewed under the supervision of the New York Missionary Society, representing nearly all the churches. Next year the Northern Missionary Society was formed and shared in the work. In 1800 the General Assembly determined to enter this field. Collections were taken, missionaries appointed, and good results secured. In 1818 the United Foreign Missionary Society, representing the Presbyterian, Reformed Dutch, and Associate Reformed Churches, was organized "to spread the Gospel among the Indians of North America, the inhabitants of Mexico and South America, and other portions of the heathen and anti-Christian world." This Society represented the interests of the Presbyterian Church in missions until 1826, when the entire work was transferred to the American Board. There were Presbyterians, however, who desired to prosecute foreign missions under Presbyterian auspices, and in 1831 the Western Foreign Missionary Society was formed by the Synod of Pittsburg, which established missions among the Indians, in India, and in Africa. In 1837, the work was handed over to a Board organized by the General Assembly. The next year the Church was divided, and the New School branch continued to contribute to the American Board, while the Old School Assembly carried on its work through the Board formed in 1837. When the re-union took place, in 1870, the united Church supported the Presbyterian Board.

The Board formerly consisted of 120 members, represented by an Executive Committee of persons residing in or near New York City, where the offices of the Board are maintained. In 1870 the Board was reduced to fifteen members, and there is no executive committee. There are four Corresponding Secretaries who, with the Treasurer, prepare the business for the Board, proposing a solution for every question, which the Board may or may not adopt, as it sees fit.

The earliest missions of the Board were among the North American Indians, as already indicated. These are now regarded as within the home mission field.

Taking up the missions of the Board in a geographical rather than a chronological order, we will first describe the fields in the Western world. Owing to the successful work among the Mexican population of the United States, carried on for many years by a woman, Miss Matilda Rankin, the Board entered Mexico in 1872, and found several congregations in the capital ready for its guiding hand. It began at once to prepare natives for the ministry and gradually pushed its work out into the surrounding country. Zacatecas, occupied in 1873, became the center of a sphere of operations in Northern Mexico.

The Board was attracted to Guatemala in 1882 by the expulsion of the Jesuits and the proclamation of religious liberty. At first the work was in English; subsequently Spanish missions were established. No other Protestant missions had been undertaken in the Republic.

The first Presbyterian mission in South America was opened in Buenos Ayres in 1853, but abandoned in 1859. The oldest existing mission of the Board was begun in the United States of Colombia in 1856, at Bogota. The opposition of the Roman priesthood has been very strong, and the work has been difficult. A second mission, at Barranquilla, was established in 1888. The Chili mission, now conducted by the Board, was received in 1873 from the American and Foreign Christian Union, an undenominational organization in New York City which gave up its work some years ago. The Chili mission has centers at Santiago, Valparaiso and Concepcion. The Rev. Ashbel Green Simonton began missionary work in the capital of Brazil in 1859. While studying Portuguese he taught English. His first congregation consisted of two of his pupils, his second of three. Gradually the number of hearers increased, and the gospel was preached in other towns in the province with good results. Sao

Paulo, in Southern Brazil, was occupied as a second center in 1863. A very important educational work is carried on. Union with the churches of the Southern Presbyterian Board was accomplished in 1889, and there are several presbyteries and a Synod of Brazil. Of the twenty provinces, twelve are represented in the Synod.

In Africa the Board has two missions: one, in Liberia, begun in 1833 at Monrovia and extended to the Kroo Coast and in the Vey and Bassa country, and organized into the Presbytery of Western Africa in 1848; the other—Gaboon—received from the American Board in 1870 and added to the Corisco mission. The latter is an offshoot of the Liberian mission. The territory occupied by the mission is partly under French, partly under German and partly under Portuguese control. This adds to the difficulty of the work of the missionaries, who minister to a superstitious, ignorant and polygamous people. In the interior some of them are or have been cannibals.

Both the Syrian and Persian missions were received from the American Board. The former dates from 1818, the latter from 1829. In Syria education for both sexes has proved a strong and successful missionary arm. Good training is given, and in the theological seminary young men are fitted for the ministry. The Syrian Protestant College, though independent of the Board, has made Beirut an important center of Protestant influence. The

mission in Persia is to the Nestorians, who consti-
tute a branch of the Eastern Church and, like other
Oriental Christians, need the gospel. Urumiah,
Tabriz, Hamadan, and other places, are occupied.

The Rev. John C. Lowrie, afterward to become
Corresponding Secretary of the Board, was sent to
India by the Western Society in 1833, with the Rev.
Wm. Reed, and they established a mission in Lodi-
ana, near the border of the Punjab, in the Northwest
Provinces. From Lodiana the work was carried
into the Punjab and into South India. Several of
the missionaries fell in the mutiny.

Siam was occupied in 1840, but little could be
done until after the death of the king, in 1851.
The new king had been under the instruction of a
missionary of the American Board, and at once
adopted a liberal policy. The first convert was not
baptized until 1859; but publication, educational and
medical work was successful, and the mission is
prosperous. A station was established in the Laos
country in 1867. For a time persecution was severe,
but religious liberty was secured in 1878.

The first year of its organization, 1837, the Presbyterian Board sent two missionaries to work
among the Chinese in Singapore. In 1843 the mission was transferred to China. There are now three
missions, known as the Central, including Ningpo,
Shanghai, Hangchau, Suchau and Nanking, the
Shantung, comprising Tungchau, Chefu, Chenan-fu
and other stations, and the Peking.

The Japan mission was founded in 1859 by Dr. James C. Hepburn and others. Work was begun at Kanagawa, near Tokyo, in a heathen temple from which the idols were cast. Subsequently the mission was removed to Yokohama at the instance of the Japanese authorities, who did not want foreigners in the town. In 1869 the first converts were baptized, and in 1872 a period of prosperity began. In 1877 the churches under the care of several Presbyterian and Reformed Boards united in organizing the "United Church of Christ in Japan," which has a complete ecclesiastical system, with a Confession of Faith, and maintains a theological seminary for the training of students for the ministry.

A mission was established at Seoul, the capital of Korea, in 1884, and success has attended it from the first.

The annual income of the Board is between $800,- 000 and $900,000, and it has about 35,000 communicants in connection with its 115 stations and 933 out-stations, 280 male and 416 female American missionaries, and 364 churches.

SOUTHERN PRESBYTERIAN BOARD

When the Civil War separated the Presbyterian Churches, Old and New Schools, on sectional lines, the consequent formation of a new foreign board by the two Southern bodies of the Presbyterian Church in the United States was necessary. The work is under the charge of an Executive Committee, and is administered by a Corresponding Secretary, with an Assistant. There is also a Treasurer.

At the time of the separation some of the missionaries in the field were from the South. Correspondence with them resulted in some cases in an agreement to represent the Southern Board in their respective fields. The Board also adopted some of the Indian missions within the bounds of the Church and cared for them until they were turned over to the Home Board in 1889.

The Board organized a mission in China, appointing for this purpose the Rev. E. B. Inslee, who had been serving the Northern Board at Hangchau. The mission now includes four stations: Hangchau, Suchau, Chinkiang and Tsing-Kiang-pu.

Miss Ronzone, as an appointee of the Board, began educational work in Naples, Italy, in 1867, and subsequently removed to Milan.

In 1868 several missionaries were sent to Brazil, where the Board now has three missions—Southern, Northern and Interior. These missions have achieved encouraging results, especially that in the State or Province of Minas-Geraes, in the interior.

A mission begun in Mexico, across the Texas border, in 1874, has been gradually extended.

Two churches were organized in Cuba in 1890 and 1891—one in Havana, the other in Santa Clara.

A mission to the Greeks in Macedonia was begun at Salonica in 1874, and has been prosecuted with varied results.

The Japan mission was begun in 1885 by two missionaries. The Board has four stations. Its churches belong to the United Church of Christ in Japan.

Convinced that duty required it to do something for the redemption of Africa the Board appointed, in 1890, a white and a colored minister to establish a mission in the Congo country. The colored minister, W. H. Sheppard, had been educated in the Tuscaloosa Theological Seminary established by the Church for colored students. They chose as their field of operations the Upper Congo and its tributary, the Kassai.

The Southern Board, with 40 stations and 126 out-stations, has 2,948 communicants on its mission fields, gathered into 34 churches. Its annual income is between $140,000 and $150,000.

UNITED PRESBYTERIAN BOARD

This Church was formed in 1858 by a union of the Associate Presbyterian and Associated Reformed Churches. Each of these Presbyterian branches had conducted foreign missions on its own account, and a new Board was organized in 1859. The Board consists of nine members chosen by the General Assembly, which also appoints the Corresponding Secretary. The Board controls the foreign missions of the Church.

Formerly the Board had missionaries in Trinidad, Syria, China, Egypt and India. For some years it has conducted its whole foreign operations in the last two fields, in which it has large and prosperous interests.

The mission in India was begun by the Associate Church at Sialkot, in the Punjab. It has been extended to include eight districts. The methods used to advance the work are the evangelistic, the educational, the zenana and the medical.

The Egyptian mission also came to the Board after it had been organized. The first missionary arrived in Cairo in 1854. The Khedive at that time, Saïd Pasha, was a liberal minded ruler and did not oppose the new mission. The mission was reinforced and in a short time there was a Presbytery of Egypt. The field of operations was chiefly among the Copts, a corrupt body of Oriental Christians. Both Moslems and Copts, outside of Cairo and Alexandria, opposed the missionaries. Mission schools and Christian publications were effective in rooting and developing gospel truths. The first native Protestant Church was organized in Cairo in 1863. The work was gradually extended up the Nile, and has become very prosperous.

The Board has in its two missions 60 churches, with 7,940 communicants. Its income in 1898 was $114,000.

CUMBERLAND PRESBYTERIAN BOARD

This branch of Presbyterianism grew out of a great revival in the Cumberland Valley, in Tennessee, in the early years of the nineteenth century.

The revival movement was carried on by methods new to the Presbyterians and was accompanied by teachings which many of them regarded as erroneous. The result was a separate denomination.

As early as 1818 the Church began mission work among the Indians. The Board, which was organized in 1845, has both home and foreign work under its control. It established missions in Liberia in 1857, in Turkey in 1860, in Trinidad in 1873, each of which has been discontinued. Its present work is in Japan and Mexico. The Mexican mission was begun in 1886.

The Board has 8 churches and 802 communicants. Its annual income is above $20,000.

REFORMED PRESBYTERIAN BOARDS

The first attempts of the Reformed Presbyterian Church (Synod) to establish foreign missions failed. Its single mission at present is the Latakia, in Syria. The original purpose was to reach the Jews at Damascus or Zahleh. Later an opening was made at Latakia among the Nusairiyeh, nominally a Moslem people but really degraded worshipers of the sun and moon. There are branches at Suadea and Mersine, and also in the island of Cyprus.

Another branch of Reformed Presbyterians, distinguished as the General Synod, began a mission in India, in the Northwest Provinces, in 1836; there are twelve churches and nearly 1,200 members.

SOUTHERN BAPTIST BOARD

The organization of this Board in 1845 was due to a division of the Regular Baptists on account of slavery. The question was raised in 1844 whether a person holding slaves could be appointed as a missionary. The answer of the Board of Foreign Missions of the Triennial Convention was that such a person could not be appointed. "We can never be a party," the Board said, "to any arrangement that would imply approbation of slavery." The Southern churches adopted the original constitution of the Convention, and claimed that the Southern Convention is the proper successor of the Triennial Convention. The Southern Baptist Convention meets annually, and consists of the Board of Foreign Missions, the Board of Home Missions, and other denominational societies.

Some of the missionaries in the field elected to serve the Southern Board; notably in China, where there are now three missions—Canton, Shanghai and Shantung. The mission property in Shanghai was destroyed during the Tai-ping rebellion, but indemnity was given afterward. The mission in Shantung dates from 1860.

The Convention has an important work in Africa, begun in 1846 in Liberia. From Liberia the work was extended into the Yoruba country and to Sierra Leone. War in Yoruba and other causes led to the suspension of that mission for some years, but the field was reoccupied in 1875. The

Liberian mission was closed and Lagos became the center of operations.

The Rev. J. W. Bowen went to Rio de Janeiro, Brazil, in the service of the Board in 1860. His health failed and the mission was suspended for twelve years, when work was renewed. Flourishing stations exist at the capital, in Pernambuco, Bahia, Maceio, and Juiz de Froa, in the State of Minas-Geraes.

The Italy mission, begun in 1890, has twelve stations, including Rome, Milan, Venice, Bologna, Modena and Naples, and two stations on the island of Sardinia.

A mission to Japan was planned as early as 1860, when three missionaries were appointed. Two were prevented from going by the outbreak of the Civil War; one sailed, but never reached his destination. Two missionaries were sent out in 1889, and a station was established at Kobe.

The annual income of the Board is about $125,000. On the various fields it has 102 churches, with 4,760 members.

FREEWILL BAPTIST SOCIETY

Free or Freewill Baptists differ from Regular Baptists respecting the distinctive doctrines of Calvinism, but immerse on confession of faith. They organized the Freewill Baptist Foreign Missionary Society in 1832, under the influence of inspiring letters from English General Baptist missionaries, and the first mission of the Society was established in India in 1835, when four missionaries, including two women, were sent out. The first station was at Sumbalpur, in the hill district of Orissa. Sumbalpur proved to be unhealthy and it was abandoned for Balasore, in the same district. The work was successfully prosecuted, and other districts were occupied. The Santhals, a hill tribe, very degraded, were effectually reached by Mr. Phillips, one of the first missionaries, who reduced their spoken language to a written one. There are twelve churches in connection with this mission, with 791 communicants. The income of the Society is about $26,000.

BOARD OF MISSIONS OF THE METHODIST EPISCOPAL CHURCH, SOUTH

The division in the Methodist Episcopal Church in 1844 led to the organization of the Methodist Episcopal Church, South, in 1845, and to a Board of Missions in 1846, when the first General Conference was held. Originally both the home and foreign fields were under the direction of one society. The work was divided in 1866, but reunited in 1870. The constitution was again so changed in 1874 by the General Conference that the Board has charge of all foreign missions and of such domestic missions as are not under the care of annual conferences.

The Board consists of twenty-five managers,

with a president, vice president, and three secretaries. The Bishops are members *ex officio*. The Board meets annually to determine what fields shall be occupied, the number of persons to be employed in each, to make appropriations, and to apportion to the conferences the amounts to be raised. Each annual conference provides for the work within its bounds and has a board auxiliary to the general board.

The first work of the Board was among the Negroes and Indians, and large results were achieved in both fields.

Dr. Charles Taylor laid the foundations of the first foreign mission in Shanghai, China, in 1848. The work opened auspiciously, but was interrupted by sickness of the missionaries and the Tai-ping rebellion. In 1854 a new start was made, but war, sickness and death supervened, and little was accomplished until 1860, when reinforcements were sent out. Trials and reverses continued until 1879, when a period of encouragement and growth began. Connected with the mission for some years were the Rev. Young J. Allen and Dr. J. W. Lambuth.

The conversion of an educated Mexican, Alijo Hernandez, who became an effective preacher to Mexicans on the Texan border, led to the opening of a mission in the City of Mexico, in 1873. Other cities and towns were occupied, and in 1886 the Central Mexico Mission Conference was organized. There is also a Mexican Border Mission

Conference which was created in the same year, and includes churches on both sides the border, in Texas and in Mexico.

A mission in Brazil was begun in 1875, in the province of Sao Paulo. Two years later a station was established in the capital.

In 1886 Dr. J. W. Lambuth, who had been connected with the mission in China, was appointed, with W. R. Lambuth, also in China, and O. A. Dukes, to begin mission work in Japan. They chose Kobe as a center. The mission was successful from the first.

The Board has 216 churches with 8,298 communicants in its various fields. Its income in 1898 was nearly $355,000.

PROTESTANT EPISCOPAL MISSIONARY SOCIETY

The Protestant Episcopal Church conducts its operations in both the home and foreign fields through one Society. The Domestic and Foreign Missionary Society was instituted in 1820, but comparatively little was done in the next ten years. A lay teacher had been sent to Africa and two clergymen to Greece. These were the first missionaries of the Church. They were commissioned in 1830.

At the session of the General Convention of the Church, which is triennial, the Bishops and dep-. uties, together with the Board of Managers and the Treasurers of the Society, sit as a Board of

Missions. This Board elects a Board of Managers, consisting of fifteen clergymen and fifteen laymen, of which board the Bishops and Treasurers are members *ex officio*. A committee consisting of eight laymen and seven clergymen, from the Board of Managers, acts in an executive capacity.

The mission in Greece was intended to awaken and instruct, but not to proselyte, nominal Christians. The work as now conducted is entirely educational. The schools are in Athens.

The China mission was begun in 1835, among the Chinese in Batavia, on the island of Java. Five years later Amoy, in China, was occupied, but was abandoned in the following year for Shanghai. The Rev. J. W. Boone, who began the mission in Amoy, was made Missionary Bishop, the first of the Anglican communion in that empire. Wuchang, in Hupeh province, was occupied as an important center in 1868, and there are now many stations in Northern and Central China, where educational, evangelistic and medical work is carried on.

The Rev. C. M. Williams and the Rev. J. Liggins, sent out in 1859, were the first Protestant missionaries, it is said, to settle in Japan. The first baptism was reported in 1866. In 1874 Japan was constituted a separate missionary jurisdiction, and Bishop Williams, who had exercised episcopal supervision from China over both fields, became the first Bishop of Japan. The chief centers of missionary work are Tokyo and Osaka.

The mission in Hayti, in charge of the Rev. J. T. Holly, was received from the American Church Missionary Society in 1865. Nine years later Dr. Holly was consecrated Bishop of Hayti.

The African mission is in Liberia. It has been a missionary bishopric since 1850. The principal tribes reached are the Grebos, the Bassas and the Veys.

The Society has 61 churches in its foreign fields, with 4,880 communicants, and received in 1898 $281,000.

AMERICAN BIBLE SOCIETY

Organized in 1816 to print and circulate the Scriptures, the American Bible Society has occupied both the home and foreign fields. It is undenominational, and is supported in part by collections taken in the evangelical churches and in part by proceeds of its sales, and from other sources. It has been the greatest possible help to the foreign missionary societies, printing versions of the Scriptures in various languages and circulating them by its own agencies, appropriating annually supplies for the use of the missions. It works in entire harmony with the missionary societies. The versions it has published, either of the whole or portions of the Bible, have been very numerous. Those of the New Testament alone number more than four score. Its operations have extended to all the fields where American missionaries have labored. One of its agencies is for Spanish South

America; another, the Levant, is for Turkey, Eastern Roumelia, part of Bulgaria, Syria and Egypt. This agency reaches many races and circulates the Bible in many languages. It is printed in Arabic, Turkish (in three characters), Armenian (in three dialects), Greek (in two), Kurdish, Persian, Syriac (ancient and modern), Hebrew, Judeo-Spanish, Bulgarian, Slavic, Roumanian, Croatian, Russian and all the languages of Europe. There is also an agency for China and one for Japan and Korea, not to mention other countries. The value of the work done by the Society in 1898 was $266,000.

OTHER SOCIETIES OF THE UNITED STATES

Almost every denomination has shown its concern for the evangelization of the world by striving to support one or more missionaries in the foreign field. In some instances, where the income is small, the work is done through the society or board of a larger denomination with whose principles and doctrines there is more or less agreement. But many bodies of less than ten thousand members maintain their own foreign mission.

I. The Disciples of Christ is one of the larger denominations, having over a million of members. It has grown recently with wonderful rapidity, having almost doubled its numbers in the last ten or twelve years. It owes its origin to Alexander Campbell and other Baptists in the beginning of the nineteenth century. Campbell was originally a

Scotch Presbyterian. He became a Baptist after he arrived in this country, and left the Baptists to found a denomination which should have no creed but the Bible, and no divisive name or principle. It was hoped that a basis would be found for the union of all believers in Christ. The Disciples baptize by immersion for the remission of sins, and administer the communion every Sunday. Because of the extent of its home work the denomination did not enter the foreign field until the last quarter of the century. Its foreign missionary society was organized in 1875. Its first field was Denmark. From Denmark the work spread to Sweden and Norway. In 1879 a mission to Turkey was begun which has attained large proportions, with stations in many places. Work was begun in the central provinces of India in 1882, in Japan in 1883, and in China in 1884. The denomination is also represented in Great Britain, Australia, and other countries. It reports 63 churches in its foreign fields, 1,426 communicants, and its income is considerably above $100,000.

II. The Lutheran communion embraces in its various divisions in this country more than a million and a half of communicants. It has been chiefly occupied in caring for immigrants from Lutheran countries in Europe, who have come in great numbers. Three of the general bodies, the General Synod, which is the oldest, and the General Council, which is one of the largest, and the United

Synod of the South, have missions abroad. The Foreign Missionary Society of the General Synod was organized in 1837. Its first mission was opened in India in 1842, in Guntur, in coöperation with the American Board, but this plan was abandoned at the end of the first year. The mission has been well supported and has been prosperous. Educational, evangelistic, medical and zenana work has been done at several stations. The Muhlenberg Mission, in Africa, was begun in 1859 in Liberia. To the educational and evangelistic arms was added an industrial feature, which has been very successful in giving the natives a knowledge of systematic farming and of the useful trades. The income of the society is upward of $42,000.

The General Council began foreign mission work in 1869 when it received from the General Synod two stations in Southern India, the Rajahmundry and Samulcotta. This mission is supported at an annual cost of about $20,000.

The United Synod of the South has an important work in Japan, begun in 1892.

III. The United Brethren in Christ, a denomination of Methodistic usages and principles formed at the beginning of the century by Germans, organized its Home, Frontier and Foreign Missionary Society in 1853, and established its first foreign mission among the Sherbro people in West Africa, where it has a large and prosperous work. The Society also has missions in Bavaria, in Germany, and in China and Japan, begun in 1889. It has 57 churches and 6,056 communicants in its foreign fields. Its income is about $42,000 a year.

IV. The Methodist Protestant Church did some foreign missionary work before it organized its own board in 1882. It has an important mission in Japan, at Yokohama, Fusiyama and Nagoya.

V. The Free Methodist Church has missions in Japan and India with six stations and two out-stations, four churches, and 68 communicants.

VI. The American Wesleyans have one foreign mission, in Freetown, West Africa.

VII. The Evangelical Association, a Methodistic organization resulting from evangelistic work among the Germans at the beginning of the century by Albright and others, has had a missionary society since 1839. Its first fields were at home and in Canada. In 1850 it began work in Germany, and later in Switzerland and Japan.

VIII. The Christian Church, a body organized in the early years of the present century, on the basis of no creed but the Bible, no divisive title, and the unity of believers, has had a foreign board since 1886. It has one foreign mission, in Japan, begun in 1887.

IX. The American Friends coöperate with the English Friends in missionary work in India and Syria, and have a mission in Mexico.

X. The German Evangelical Synod represents in the United States the State Church of Prussia, which was formed by the union of the Lutherans and the Reformed elements. It formerly contributed to foreign missions through societies in Germany. In 1884 it took up the work of the German Evangelical Society, which had been supported by Germans of several denominations. There was a mission in India, at Bisrampore, which has become a center of influence. There are four churches with 807 members.

XI. The Associate Reformed Synod of the South, a small body which did not enter the union which made the United Presbyterian Church, has a mission in Mexico. It began its foreign missionary work in 1875, when it sent a missionary to Egypt. On her death it shifted its field of operations to Tamaulipas, Mexico.

XII. The African Methodist Episcopal Church, the largest colored Methodist body in the United States, began missionary work in Africa in 1886, and has considerable interests in Sierra Leone and in South Africa. The Church also has missions in Hayti.

XIII. The German Baptists, or Dunkards, zealous and peculiar Bible Christians who came from Germany in the eighteenth century and are now divided into four branches, have had mission work in Denmark and Sweden for many years, the former begun in 1875, the latter in 1885. It is the conservative and more numerous branch that supports these missions.

XIV. One branch of the Mennonites, known as the General Conference, has a foreign missionary society which began work among the Indians in 1880. It has no mission abroad.

XV. The Seventh Day Baptists, one of the oldest and also one of the smallest denominations in this country, have a mission in Shanghai, China, begun in 1847, and missions in Belgium, Holland, and among the Jews in Austria.

XVI. The Seventh Day Adventists, a branch of the movement which was led by William Miller in the forties, are very active in missionary work, which is carried on very systematically. The foreign missions are chiefly in Christian countries, including Great Britain, Australia, various European countries, the West Indies, and Canada. They also have missions in India, China, Japan, Africa, several groups of Pacific Islands, and Mexico and South America. They have in Great Britain and Europe 5,646 members, in Australia, 1,713, and in other foreign countries, exclusive of Canada, 1,800.

XVII. The National Baptist Convention, representing colored Baptists, has a foreign missionary board located at Louisville. The colored Baptists have done more or less missionary work in Africa and in Hayti.

CANADIAN FOREIGN MISSION SOCIETIES

There are six foreign boards or societies in Canada: one each for the Congregationalists,

Methodists, Presbyterians, and Episcopalians, and two for the Baptists.

I. The Congregationalists of Canada formed a foreign missionary society in 1881, supporting missionaries of the American Board in Turkey and Japan. In 1886 a missionary was sent to Africa.

II. The Methodist Church of Canada has had a missionary society since 1824. It is both home and foreign in its scope. It has done much work among the Indians, with very encouraging results. It has a mission in Bermuda, but its most important foreign work is in Japan. This mission was begun in 1873, in Tokyo. There are several stations and a considerable body of communicants. The society raises for its foreign work about $42,000 a year.

III. The Presbyterian Church of Canada is the result of the union of four bodies in 1875. The united Church consolidated the existing mission interests in one board. It has a mission in the New Hebrides, which is carried on in coöperation with the missions of Scottish Churches, one in Trinidad, one in Central India, one in Formosa, and one in Honan, China. The city of Indore is the center of the work in India. The Formosa mission has been made famous by the heroic work of the Rev. George L. Mackay, who married a Chinese woman and identified himself with the interests of the people. For a time he was severely persecuted, but he won the confidence of the inhabitants, and the mission has been very successful. The Honan field was occupied strongly in 1889. The society has large mission interests among the Indians.

IV. The Church of England in Canada organized a missionary society in 1883. What it does in the foreign field is done through other organizations.

V. The Baptists of Canada raised money for foreign missions long before they maintained missions of their own. They supported missionaries in connection with the American Baptist Missionary Union. In 1867 the Baptists of Ontario and Quebec sent out their first missionaries to the heathen. They went to Madras and Burma, laboring under the direction of the American Baptist Missionary Union. Two independent organizations were formed in 1873, one by the Maritime Provinces and the other by the Provinces of Ontario and Quebec. They unite in support of the mission in the Northern Telugu country in India.

CHAPTER X

WOMEN'S FOREIGN MISSIONARY SOCIETIES

EVERY denomination having foreign missions has, with few exceptions, one women's missionary society or more. There were such societies as early as 1800, although they did not work specifically for foreign missions. After the American Board was organized women's societies auxiliary to it were formed, one as early as 1812, and Baptist, Presbyterian and Methodist societies came into existence before 1820. None of these societies carried on operations abroad under its own direction. They collected money and turned it over to the regular societies of their respective churches. It was not until 1834 that women's societies were organized for work in the mission field. In that year, in response to an appeal from the Rev. David Abeel, of China, for women missionaries to reach the women of India and China, the Society for Promoting Female Education in the East was created in England. Other societies of the same kind came speedily into existence, including one for the Wesleyan Church, one for the Free and one for the Established Church of Scotland.

The first society of the kind in the United States was formed in 1861 on undenominational lines. It

(14)   209

was called the Woman's Union Missionary Society for Heathen Lands. The Society's first missionary, Miss Marston, went out the same year to Burma. The sphere of operations of this society has been in India, China, and Japan. Zenana work has been the leading feature of its operations. In common with other women's societies it also carries on evangelistic, educational, and medical work, and employs many Bible women, chiefly natives.

This is the only independent and undenominational society in the United States. There are three such societies in England: the Society for Promoting Female Education in the East, already mentioned, which has missionaries in Palestine, Persia, India, China, Japan and Egypt; the Indian Female Normal School and Instruction Society, organized in 1852, which has schools, and does zenana, Bible and medical work in India; and the British Syrian Mission Schools and Bible Work among the neglected women and children in Syria.

Denominational women's societies in the United States exist in most of the Churches. The Congregational Churches have four such societies, representing various sections of the country. Two of them were organized in 1868, one in Boston the other in Chicago; there is also a Board on the Pacific Coast and one in the Sandwich Islands. The sphere of the latter is in the Hawaiian group and in Micronesia. The first three coöperate with the American Board in India, China, Japan, Africa,

Turkey, Mexico, and Spain. These societies maintain boarding and day schools, employ Bible women, hold evangelistic meetings, and do medical work.

The Woman's Foreign Missionary Society of the Methodist Episcopal Church was formed in 1869 in Boston. Its fields are, in the order of occupation, India, China, Mexico and South America, Japan and Africa, Italy, Bulgaria, and Korea. It conducts schools, boarding and day, does direct evangelistic work in house to house visitation, in tours and in meetings of various kinds, and has an important medical department. Its medical missionaries gain access to houses and influence in circles which would be closed to ordinary missionary work. Dr. Leonora Howard, sent to Peking in 1877, was summoned the next year to Tientsin, to attend the wife of the great Chinese statesman, Li Hung Chang. Under her treatment Lady Li recovered. The result was a pressing invitation to remain in Tientsin, the placing of a temple at her disposal for dispensary work the cost of which was met by Lady Li, and finally a hospital built by the Society.

There are several Boards in the Presbyterian Church, three of which were organized in 1870. They have missions among the Indians, in Mexico, Guatemala, South America, West Africa, Syria, Persia, India, Siam, Laos, China, Japan and Korea. Their appropriations and appointments are always submitted to the regular Foreign Board at New York.

Among other women's foreign societies are those of the Methodist Episcopal Church, South, organized in 1878; of the Reformed (Dutch) Church, organized in 1875; of the Cumberland Presbyterian Church, organized in 1880; of the United Presbyterian Church, organized in 1883; of the Northern Baptists, organized in 1871 (four sectional societies); of the Southern Baptist Convention, organized in 1884; of the Protestant Episcopal Church, organized in 1871; of the Lutheran General Synod, organized in 1879. There are also similar bodies in Canada, in connection with the various Churches.

In England there is the Ladies' Auxiliary of the Wesleyan Methodist Missionary Society, organized in 1858; the Ladies' Association for the Promotion of Female Education Among the Heathen, organized in 1865 as auxiliary to the Society for the Propagation of the Gospel, Church of England; Ladies' Association, auxiliary to the Baptist Missionary Society; Ladies' Committee of the London Missionary Society, organized in 1875; Woman's Missionary Association, Presbyterian, organized in 1878; Zenana Missionary Society, auxiliary to the Church Missionary Society, Church of England.

In Scotland there are three women's societies in connection with the Church of Scotland: one for general missionary and zenana work, organized in 1837, and two for educational and other work among the Jews; three in connection with the Free Church: one for female education in India and

South Africa, organized in 1837, another for work
among the Jews, and a third for work on the Continent; a Zenana Mission and a Kaffrarian Society
in connection with the United Presbyterian Church;
and a Society in connection with the Episcopal
Church of Scotland.

In Ireland there is an association for work among
the women of the East, organized in 1873.

Two women's societies are reported from Germany: the Berlin Women's Missionary Association,
more than sixty years old, which has work in India
and in Jerusalem, and the Berlin Women's Mission
for China. There are other women's societies on
the Continent, notably one in Stockholm, Sweden.
These societies operate in China and in Africa.

CHAPTER XI

The Mission Fields of the World

The peoples of the earth among whom Protestant missionaries are laboring may be divided into five classes, as follows: I. Papal, Oriental Christian and Protestant; II. Mohammedan; III. Jewish; IV. Asiatic Heathen; V. Uncivilized.

I. PAPAL, ORIENTAL CHRISTIAN AND PROTESTANT POPULATIONS

1. Missions in Papal Countries. The Roman Catholic Church is not always and everywhere the same, notwithstanding its old Latin motto to that effect. It is very different in Protestant countries like England, the United States and Germany, from what it is in Italy, Spain and South American countries. It is not tolerant of other forms of religion where it enjoys control, and would exclude them all by force if it could. In Latin lands—Italy, Spain and Portugal in Europe and Spanish countries in America—the church has made little progress toward a higher and more spiritual Christianity. The example of the priests is often a reproach to religion and morals, and the people are superstitious and believe that observance of rites and ceremonies and oft-repeated prayers to the

Virgin and the saints will atone for evil lives. Protestant missionaries have had to encounter the most
strenuous opposition and every form of persecution
which the state would allow. A deep-seated prej-
udice must first be overcome before the people can
be reached and influenced for good.

In America, Canadian Churches are at work
among the French Catholics of the Dominion;
many societies of the United States, including our
own, among the Romanists of Mexico, where there
has been complete religious liberty under the
government of President Diaz; Methodist, Presbyterian, Baptist, and other societies of the United
States, including the American Bible Society, and
the South American Missionary Society of England, the Moravians and others in the various
countries of South America, except Bolivia, where
no missionary work seems to have been attempted;
Methodist, Presbyterian, and other societies in
Cuba and Porto Rico, since the late Spanish war,
the Baptists and Southern Methodists having made
beginnings in Cuba before the war. In Mexico
considerable success has attended missionary work.
The Government confiscated and sold churches,
monasteries and other ecclesiastical property, which
the Catholic Church had accumulated, and Protestant congregations are occupying these buildings.
A reform movement, led by natives, and organized
into a separate Church under the auspices of the
Protestant Episcopal Church, has a considerable

following. In South America the missionaries have less freedom and work under greater difficulties. Progress, however, is beginning to be made. The history of the attempts made by the South American Society to reach the degraded peoples of Tierra del Fuego and Patagonia is tragic, and the blood of the martyrs was not shed in vain.

All Italy has been open to Protestant missionaries since the kingdom was reunited. The end of the temporal power of the Pope and the removal of the seat of the government of King Victor Emanuel from Turin to Rome was hailed by the Protestant world as well as the political as a most significant event, and missionary societies prepared almost immediately to take advantage of it. Protestantism was already represented in Italy by the heroic little Church of the Waldensians. Missions were established in the papal city and in other centers by our own society, and by various other American and English societies, including the Wesleyan. The results have not been large. The field has proved a hard one. Prejudices are strong, and Protestant requirements seem rigorous to people so long accustomed to a form of religion imposing few moral restraints.

Spain, like Italy, is stubborn ground for missionary endeavor. The American Board and several English societies have interests there which are developing very slowly.

France, though dominantly Roman Catholic,

also recognizes and supports other religions, in-cluding the Reformed, representing the old Hugue-notic Protestants, and the Jews. The Reformed Church is pervaded with Rationalism. There is the Free Church, a small Protestant body, and missions conducted by the English Wesleyans, by a few small American societies and, most important of all, by what is known as the McAll mission, an undenominational movement supported by Prot-estants in the United States, England and Scot-land.

Austria is almost wholly Roman Catholic, ex-cepting Hungary—where there is a large Reformed element, generally Rationalistic. The American Board has missions in the empire, and so have the Moravians. There is religious toleration but not religious liberty, and missionaries are restricted in their operations.

2. MISSIONS AMONG ORIENTAL CHRISTIANS. There are some half dozen or more ancient Churches in Eastern lands, usually called Oriental or Eastern Churches; including the orthodox Greek Church—which is the State Church in Russia and in Greece—the Armenians, the Nestorians, the Jacobites, the Copts of Egypt, and the Abyssinian Christians. The Greek Church is due to the division over the doctrine of the procession of the Spirit; the Western or Latin Christians holding that the Holy Spirit proceeds from the Father and the Son, and the Eastern or Greek Christians that

he proceeds from the Father alone. The Armenian Church is the result of an earlier division on the question of one nature and one person of Christ. They agree with the Greeks as to the procession of the Spirit and on other points, and also with Roman Catholics in several particulars. The Nestorians deny that the human and divine in Christ combined to form one nature, hence they are anti-monophysites. The Jacobites are monophysite Christians found chiefly in Syria and parts of Turkey. The Coptic is a very ancient Church of Egypt and the Abyssinian is a corrupt combination of Christian and Jewish elements.

The missions of the American Board in Turkey, of the Presbyterian Board in Syria and Persia and of our own Society in Bulgaria are chiefly to the Greeks, Armenians, Jacobites and Nestorians. Great success has attended these efforts of the American Board and the Presbyterian Board and thousands have accepted the gospel, and converted ministers of the old faiths have become pastors and active evangelists. Our mission in Northern Bulgaria has had great difficulties to meet and has but little progress to report. The Church of England, by means of what is known as the "Archbishops' Assyrian Mission" has sought to reform the Assyrian or Nestorian Christians within their own Church. These bodies of oriental Christians have suffered great persecutions by the Turks. The most recent, a few years ago, was so violent and bloody that the Christian world stood aghast, but for political reasons declined to interfere. Christians, both of the old faiths and of the new introduced by missionaries, were given their choice of the acceptance of Islam or the sword, with unspeakable degradation for the women of their households. In the presence of such a horrible menace they proved that they were made of the stuff of martyrs. They would not deny the Christ, and fell in awful slaughter, leaving their women to even a worse fate. Constantinople is a center of evangelical influence in connection with the educational and publication work of the American Board and Bible distribution by the American Bible Society. Among the Copts in Egypt the United Presbyterians of the United States have carried on a successful evangelical and educational work, assisted by several English societies. Nothing has yet been done for the Abyssinians, who are not accessible in their own country.

3. MISSIONS IN PROTESTANT COUNTRIES. These are in Europe. Attention was drawn to the need of a more spiritual and earnest type of Christianity in Germany and Scandinavia by natives of those countries who visited the United States and got into a warmer religious atmosphere. Consequently, extensive missionary operations are carried on by our own Society in Germany, Switzerland, and the Scandinavian countries, and by the Baptists in the same lands, and also by the United Brethren in

Christ and the Evangelical Association in Germany. We also have missions among the Finns of Russia and in St. Petersburg. The results are regarded as helpful in preparing men and women for an active Christian life and in awakening a more earnest spirit in the old Churches.

II. MISSIONS TO MOHAMMEDAN POPULATIONS.

Islam, or the religion of Mohammed, was a strong protest against the polytheistic systems that prevailed when the prophet arose. It declares that there is but one God, and Mohammed is his prophet. It inculcates temperance, but practices polygamy, begets an intense devotional spirit, but is unmindful of some of the virtues and makes its converts by the sword. It has followers to the number perhaps of 175,000,000. These are found in the Turkish Empire, whose Sultan is the head of the faith; in Arabia and Persia; in Morocco, Algeria, the Great Desert, the Soudan, and other African countries; in India, Afghanistan, Baluchistan, and countries of Central Asia, and the Malay Peninsula and archipelago. Little or no missionary work has been done among the Moslems of Turkey by the American Board, as the Government would not allow it. Evangelical influences have in a few cases reached them, however, but they could not openly avow a change of religion without danger of being suddenly and secretly cut off. A number of converts known to the missionaries disappeared, some years ago, and never were seen or heard of again. Moslems have purchased the Scriptures and it is believed that the great work of the American Board has impressed them, and that, if they were free to renounce Islam, Christianity might make converts among them. The missionaries working in Persia and Arabia are under the same limitations. In Egypt direct work is possible among the Moslems, and the United Presbyterian Board of the United States and the Church Missionary Society of England have in their schools many hundred Moslem boys and girls who are receiving a Christian training. One society is operating in Morocco. There are in India about 60,000,000 Mohammedans. They are, of course, accessible to missionary influences. The universities, various Christian schools, medical missions, and the personal character and work of the missionaries continue to impress the Moslem that there is truth in Christianity. Great numbers however have not embraced it. Among the effective ministers in our own Conferences in India are men won from Islam. How many there are among our lay members we have no way of determining. The greatest successes have been among the Mohammedans of Java and Sumatra. Islam is said to be making fewer converts from the heathen there than Christianity is from Islam. The missionaries seem to have found a direct way to the hearts of these people.

The foundations have been laid for missionary

work among the followers of the false prophet. The Arabic Bible will plead the cause of Christianity powerfully. Political influences of a disintegrating character at work in Turkey and Persia may make Mohammedan fields, now among the hardest before the Christian missionary, easier and more fruitful in the near future.

III. MISSIONS TO THE JEWS

The Jew is everywhere. He is the truest of cosmopolites. He is at home in every country and among every people. Christianity does not have to go to him, he comes to it. There are supposed to be over 7,000,000 of the representatives of the race into which Christ was born, the bulk of whom are in European countries. Though singularly tenacious of their racial pecularities and of their religion, they are coming into the Christian Church constantly, here and there one. We have organized in the United States no special agencies to reach them, but our own Society, with others, has one or more missionaries working among them. In Great Britain there are a number of societies established specially for the conversion of Jews, and their fields are in Europe, Asia and Africa.

IV. MISSIONS TO THE HEATHEN OF ASIA

In Asia. the cradle of civilization and of Christianity, we find the greatest and densest heathen populations in the world. China, India, Japan, Korea and Indo-China have 750,000,000 people, according to the latest estimates; more than one half of the population of the globe. Not all of these are heathen, but when we deduct the sixty or seventy millions of Mohammedans and the Christians, who do not rise into the millions, we still have a mass of 675,000,000 or 680,000,000 persons who "in their blindness, bow down to wood and stone." The figures are appalling, and so are the facts of social, moral and religious conditions. The religions represented are chiefly Confucianism, Hinduism, Buddhism, Taoism and Shintoism. But it will be most convenient to consider this vast subject by fields rather than by religions, making these divisions: 1. India; 2. China; 3. Japan; 4. Korea; 5. French Indo-China and Siam.

1. MISSIONS TO THE HEATHEN IN INDIA. We include under this term India, Ceylon and Burma, over which British rule extends, excepting Nepaul, and several native and foreign States. The people of India are divided as to race, on the basis of language, as follows: 1, Aryan stock, covering most of India, except the lower end of the peninsula, and including the Hindi, the Bengali, the Marathi, the Sindhi and the Punjabi tongues; 2, the Dravidian, covering the southern part of the peninsula, and including the Tamil, the Telugu, the Kanarese; 3, Kolarian, covering minute areas and embracing the hill tribes of Central India; 4, Burmo-Tibetan,

covering Nepaul and Burma. Each of these groups of languages contains numerous dialects: the Dravidian, twelve principal variations; the Kolarian, nine; the Burmo-Tibetan, twenty; and the Aryan a vast number, making in all some 300 dialects spoken in India. In religion, the people may be classified as Hindus, constituting four fifths of the population; Mohammedans, 60,000,000; Buddhists, about 3,-500,000; Sikhs and Jains 1,750,000, and Parsis 75,000. Hinduism, with its trinity, its doctrine of transmigration, its Brahminic code of ceremonies and observances, and its intricate and devilish caste system, holds its followers in the most abject religious and social bondage. As Dr. Duff said of it, "Unlike Christianity, which is all spirit and life, Hinduism is all letter and death." Buddhism is a more humane system than Hinduism, but is agnostic or atheistic, has no doctrine of definite personal immortality, and is a pessimistic system. Sikhism is a modification of Hinduism, Jainism is a mixture of Buddhism and Hinduism, and Parsiism is the religion of Zoroaster.

The Danish missionaries, Ziegenbalg and Plütschau, were the first Protestants to carry Christianity to the caste-ridden heathen of India. They went to Tranquebar in South India in 1705; but little was done until English control became firm and strong and Parliament, in 1814, allowed Christian evangelization to be undertaken. Almost all the great missionary societies, American, British and Continental, are represented in India. The first missions of the American Board and the American Baptist Missionary Union were begun in that great country, with which we include Burma. The Methodist Episcopal Church came much later into the field, its mission having been founded by Dr. Wm. Butler in 1856. We have now, as the result of that modest beginning, five Annual Conferences and one Mission Conference, and between 75,000 and 80,000 communicants. For many years missions in India had little encouragement. Among the first to receive the gospel were those of the lower castes and outcasts; but the leaven has worked its way upward and even the intensely religious Brahmin has been affected by it. The relief given to sufferers by the great famines has powerfully impressed the heathen mind, and the most notable ingatherings of the Church Missionary and other societies followed one of these exhibitions of Christian love and care. Christianity is growing daily in influence and power and is slowly but surely undermining the old religious systems, which for so many centuries have stood as barriers to all social, religious and intellectual progress.

2. MISSIONS TO THE HEATHEN IN CHINA. China is the most populous country of the globe. It is credited with over 400,000,000 people, inhabiting an area considerably larger than the United States. It is a very ancient country, with a very long history. Events are traced back to 2205 B. C.

Before that were legendary and mythological periods, the latter including the creation of the world, by Pwanku, with a mallet and chisel. The country has been variously known as Cathay to the Persians, Seres to the Latins, by other countries in Asia as Jin, Sin, etc., and by the Chinese themselves as Tien Ha, signifying the world.

China was practically closed to foreigners until the close of the war with Great Britain, in 1842, when five ports were opened first to the English and then to other nations. By the treaty of Tientsin, at the close of the second war with Great Britain, toleration of Christianity, residence of foreign ministers at Peking and freedom to travel in the empire were secured, though the terms of the treaty had to be enforced by the allied powers in 1860. The language, different from all other modern languages, has several dialects, the chief of which are the Mandarin, or Court language, the Cantonese, the Amoy and the Fuhchau dialects. There is also a book language, called the Wen-li. The three chief systems of religion are the Confucian, Taoist and Buddhist. These systems coexist without serious antagonisms. Individuals may, and do, accept all three without being deemed inconsistent. One may, however, be a Confucianist without accepting any features of the other two religions; but Taoists and Buddhists are usually also Confucianists. The body of the people may, therefore, be fairly termed Confucianists distinctively.

The worship of ancestors, the real religion of the Chinese, is part of the Confucian system; next to this reverence for departed parents is the respect paid to the influence of wind and water, Fung Shwui. Sacrifices are made to rain, wind, thunder, etc., and the religion of the people is characterized by superstition and fear. Things living and things dead, spirits, the winds, water, stars, eclipses, unlucky days, etc., enter into the thoughts of the people and control their actions. There is no caste, but class distinctions are recognized, the greatest honor being paid to the scholar; the farmer comes second, the artisan third and the trader fourth. St. Thomas, according to tradition, first preached the gospel to the Chinese. The Nestorians are known to have been in the empire as early as 505 A. D. The Catholics began missionary work in 1292, were subsequently expelled and began again in 1586. They made many converts and gained much influence, but were banished in 1618. Some traces of Catholicism remained when missions were renewed after the treaties which proclaimed toleration.

Robert Morrison, the first Protestant missionary to China, was sent out in 1806 by the London Missionary Society, reaching Canton in 1807. Shortly after he had to retire to Macao; belonging to Portugal, and there prepared for missionary work. Two other missionaries were sent out by the London Society, one in 1813, the third in 1822.

The American Board was the second society to enter the field, sending the Rev. E. C. Bridgman to Canton in 1829. The Methodist was the tenth society to seek the establishment of a mission in the great empire. It was one of six societies which did this in the year 1847.

The mission centers multiplied, new provinces were gradually opened, and nearly all parts of the vast territory are now occupied. Naturally, slow progress was made for a quarter of a century or more in gaining converts. The great dislike for foreigners, the prevalent superstitions, the bitter antagonism of the literary class, the opium habit, and other difficulties, have barred the way of Christainity, but it is gradually overcoming these obstacles. In 1877 there were 13,515 communicants connected with Protestant societies; thirteen years later this number had been nearly trebled: 37,287. Christianity is surely gathering momentum, and its outlook for the twentieth century is very promising.

3. MISSIONS TO THE HEATHEN IN JAPAN. Japan is the foreign name for Dai Nippon (great dayspring). It has a population of over 41,000,000. They are a bright, enterprising people, and are sometimes called the French of Asia. They are quick to accept Western civilization, and seem to have none of the sluggishness of the Chinese. In religion, they are generally Buddhists. Shintoism is the state religion. It was doubtless founded on ancestor-worship. The great Roman Catholic,

Francis Xavier, introduced Christianity into Japan in
1549, and it obtained a considerable foothold; but it
was severely persecuted and declined in influence.
When Japan was opened by treaty in 1859, three
hundred and ten years after Xavier began his mission, Roman Catholics, Russian Orthodox and
Protestant missionaries went into the empire together. Of the Protestant missionaries, the first to
arrive were representatives of the Protestant
Episcopal Church; next, of the American Presbyterian, and, third, of the Reformed (Dutch) Church
in America. There was really little opportunity for
missionary work until after the revolution of 1868.
The language was a difficulty, the people were sunk
low in morals, and the government watchful and
suspicious. But by degrees the missionaries
secured the attention and confidence of the people,
and their work has been attended with great success.
The Presbyterian and Reformed Missions united in
organizing, in 1877, "the Church of Christ in
Japan," which is a large and very influential body.
Japan is apparently an attractive field, as a great
number of societies are represented in it. The
results have been very encouraging. The Japanese
Christian is quite independent in spirit, and has
accepted very readily the idea of self-support. The
native ministers are an able, earnest body of men,
quite ready to take the responsibility of preaching,
evangelizing and organizing, when the time shall
come for the withdrawal of the missionaries. As

indicating the readiness with which the Japanese accept Western ideas, it may be added that the government has carried the secular idea of education so far as to refuse recognition to graduates of schools in which religion is taught.

4. MISSIONS TO THE HEATHEN IN KOREA. The Hermit Kingdom, so called because it so persistently kept its doors closed to the commercial world, entered into treaty relations with the United States in 1882, and later with other nations. It has a population of about 10,500,000 of the Mongolian type. The Korean language is widely different both from the Chinese and Japanese, though the character of the former is used in writing. It has an alphabet which is said to compare favorably in many points with the best known in other countries. Formerly the Buddhist was the religion of the people, but for some centuries Confucianism has been decidedly in the ascendant. Catholicism was introduced near the end of the eighteenth century by Koreans who had become acquainted with it in Peking. It was received with favor, but was subsequently greatly persecuted, several thousand native members perishing at one time. When Korea was opened by the treaties of 1882 there were, it is estimated, not fewer than 50,000 Roman Catholics in the kingdom. The first Protestant missionary to enter upon work in Korea was Dr. N. H. Allen, of China. He arrived in the fall of 1884. Dr. R. S. Maclay, of the Methodist mission in Japan, had

visited the country previously, and as soon as his report could be acted upon Dr. Wm. B. Scranton and the Rev. H. G. Appenzeller were appointed as missionaries. They reached the field in 1885. Other societies have established missions, and the outlook is promising.

5. MISSIONS TO THE HEATHEN IN FRENCH INDO-CHINA AND SIAM. The Kingdom of Siam forms a part of the Indo-China peninsula. It has a population of nearly 6,000,000, the majority of which consists of Siamese and Shans. Their language is monosyllabic and is distinguished by tones, like the Chinese. Buddhism is the prevailing religion and it has a very strong hold upon the people. A form of Shamanism, or demon worship, also coexists with Buddhism. Dr. Karl Gutzlaff, of the Netherlands, and Mr. Tomlin of the London Missionary Society, visited Bangkok in 1828, and set to work there, appealing to America for missionaries to occupy the field. The American Board sent Dr. Abeel in 1831, but none of these missionaries remained very long. Successors to Dr. Abeel were sent out in 1834. The American Baptist Missionary Union also entered the field from Burma, and the Presbyterian Board founded a mission at Bangkok in 1848. These missions were to the Siamese. In 1867 work was begun among the Laos tribes, in the northern part of the kingdom. For a time persecution was visited upon the missionaries and converts, but since the death of the persecuting king at

Chieng-Mai, and the accession of a new king at Bangkok, toleration has been the rule. The present king of Siam is an enlightened and liberal monarch, and the missions have enjoyed the royal favor. The Presbyterian Board, at the Presbyterian reunion in 1870 in this country and the withdrawal of Presbyterian contributions to the American Board, received the missions of the latter organization in Siam. The country is now open to evangelistic effort, and the missionaries believe that bright and promising days are before them.

French Indo-China embraces Cambodia, Cochin-China, Anam and Tonkin, all under French rule. There are no missions in this section of the peninsula except those conducted by the Roman Catholic Church.

V. MISSIONS TO UNCIVILIZED HEATHEN

The countries embraced in this division are those of Africa South of the Great Desert, the Indian tribes of North and South America, and the island groups of the Pacific, the South Seas and elsewhere. The work among the Indians of the United States and Alaska is properly home mission work and need not be considered here. What is done in the Dominion of Canada and British America is done chiefly by the Canadian Churches, and by the Church of England Societies. Greenland is missionary ground of the Moravian and Danish Missionary Societies. The savages of Patagonia are being reached in some measure by the South American Missionary Society, of England. These people were so low in the scale of human intelligence that when Darwin, the celebrated naturalist, first came into contact with them, he doubted whether they were capable of being taught. They seemed to be all animal. But the patient labors of the missionaries brought results which convinced the scientist that even the Fuegians or Patagonians are capable of development, intellectually, morally and religiously.

·I. MISSIONS IN AFRICA. Africa, so far as the interior was concerned, was almost a sealed book until the explorations of Rebmann, Speke and Burton were continued and completed by Livingstone and Stanley and others. The countries on the coast line, from the Gulf of Aden on the east around the Cape of Good Hope to Senegal on the west, have long been known, and the world has had important commercial relations with them. Formerly these commercial relations often involved the exchange of goods for slaves. The United States, the West India Islands and other countries had Negro slaves in this way; but the conscience of Christian nations was aroused on this subject, and the iniquitous traffic was gradually abolished, and slavery is now everywhere at an end except among Mohammedans and savages. The African race is known in all parts of the civilized world, and enlightened peoples, like those of our own country, have had an excellent opportunity to study its capacities and characteristics. Superstitious, cruel, degraded savages, often cannibals, in their natural state, in their own continent, Negroes have come to the front rank in all that constitutes noble manhood, where the right conditions were afforded them. It is said that such was the contempt in which the early Dutch settlers of South Africa held the Hottentots, that the legend, "Dogs and Hottentots not admitted," was sometimes placed over their church doors. Yet Hottentots and Bushmen, at the bottom of the intellectual scale, have under missionary teaching and influence made good Christians and good Christian preachers and pastors. Cape Colony, the Transvaal and the Orange Free State, the former under English rule, the latter independent or semi-independent states, are European in population largely. Liberia is a republic, founded under American auspices and colonized by American Negroes. European interests are more extensive on the West Coast than on the East, and Protestant missions were early established in the countries bordering on the Gulf of Guinea. The climate was so fatal to foreigners that this portion of the continent has been called the "white man's grave." Missionary after missionary has fallen, and yet, in the spirit of the hero Cox, though perhaps a thousand have fallen Africa has not been given up. The climate has been one difficulty, the slave traffic another, the rum traffic still another and the savage superstitions a fourth. These have not been encountered in equal degree in all parts of Africa, for the interior is salubrious and parts of South Africa are reasonably healthy. In the last quarter of the nineteenth century missionary enterprise in Africa has developed wonderfully. Societies have pushed into the interior, along the great Congo River and its tributaries, and are reaching tribes unknown before Stanley's great discoveries; they have at great cost planted missions on the shores of the Victoria Nyanza, Lake Tanganyika and elsewhere in the very heart of the continent. To Stanley's appeal for missionaries for King Mtesa's people in Uganda, at the north end of Lake Victoria, the Church Missionary Society promptly responded, and its expedition marched over 800 miles, along a scarcely known caravan route, and reached its destination. Amid encouragements and discouragements, revolutions, massacres and oppression, the missionaries have labored these years, and the results already justify the immense outlay of treasure and labor and life. The kingdom is becoming a Christian kingdom, and the Spirit of God is taking the place, in the hearts of the people, of the *Lubari,* dreadful spirits of the lake. The London Society is similarly established on the shores of Lake Tanganyika and Scotch societies on those of Lake Nyassa. Every year the slave raids are being reduced, and the cruel Arab slave stealers are so hemmed in with Christian mission stations that their inhuman business is well-nigh destroyed. It is not possible to pass in review all the countries where missionary effort is seeking to evangelize and enlighten the people. The Protestant world has numerous representatives on the East and West Coasts, in the South and in the interior, preaching, teaching, healing and fitting the people for peaceful industrial pursuits. Lovedale Institution, in South Africa, is a center of light and influence, preparing men for the ministry, for teaching and for various industrial and mechanical vocations.

The partition of Africa among the European nations assures the early suppression of what remains of the terrible slave traffic, the gradual increase of peace conditions, the building of roads and telegraphs, and the commercial development of their various spheres of influence. England, Germany, and France are busy with railroad enterprises which will connect the interior with the Coast, and telegraph lines which will make it possible to flash messages from old Ujiji and the capital of Uganda to any part of the civilized world.

2. MISSIONS IN MADAGASCAR. Madagascar, a considerable island off the East Coast of Africa, deserves a separate paragraph. Its chief tribe, educated and developed by Christian missionary enterprise, had become a Christian people with a Christian government and Christian institutions. They were evangelizing the heathen tribes and constantly extending the area of Christian civilization,

when France began a war of conquest a few years ago, and subjugated the island. French policy represses Protestant endeavor and encourages Catholic enterprise. It is feared that the result will be disastrous to the work of the London Missionary Society and that of the English Society of Friends, to which belongs the honor of having won these people from heathenism and savage superstitions.

3. MISSIONS IN THE SOUTH SEAS. The islands of the South Seas have been scenes of thrilling interest in missionary history. Included in this somewhat indefinite term are the Ladrones, the Caroline, Marshall and Gilbert groups, belonging to Micronesia, and New Guinea, and the Solomon, New Hebrides, Ellice and Fiji groups, in Melanesia.

In the Micronesian groups the people are of the brown Polynesian race. When first discovered they were a fierce people. They would rob ships and kill the crew, and in some cases cannibal feasts were held. Their religion was a kind of spiritism. They were, of course, degraded and immoral, though they acquired vices from civilized visitors. Missionaries of the American Board began work in the Carolines in 1852, assisted by Hawaiians. The first five years were years of discouragement; the second five years were years of excellent results. The work was extended in the Caroline and to the Gilbert and Marshall groups, and later to the Mortlocks. Converts from Ponape inaugurated the mission in the Mortlocks. Of the 85,000 population in

Micronesia, upward of 50,000 have heard the gospel, and great social and other changes have been wrought by Christian ideas.

In Melanesia, the Fijian and New Hebridean groups deserve most particular notice. The Fijians, a cross between the Malay and Papuan or Negro types, held preëminence for cruelty, wickedness and savagery. They were fierce warriors who killed and ate their enemies, made away with aged relatives, destroyed widows, and sacrificed slaves. They were a terror to shipwrecked crews. Their chief deity was a large serpent, and the spirits of heroes and chiefs were worshiped. The Wesleyan Missionary Society of England began missionary work among them in 1835, as the result of a revival in the Friendly Islands, some of the Friendly Island converts being with the missionary party. It was a hard field, and history says that "perhaps there never was another such struggle between light and darkness, truth and error, as that which took place in the course of the Fiji mission," but the missionaries would not give up, and the kingdom of Satan had to. A moral, social and religious revolution was the result, and Fijians were among the missionaries who carried the gospel later on to New Guinea and were martyred there. In the New Hebrides, where Scotch and Canadian Presbyterians have exemplified the faithfulness and courage of the apostles of the first century, similar results have come to bless missionary labors and certify to the

power of God to change the human heart. New
Guinea is one of the later scenes of gospel triumph.
This island in size is second only to Australia. The
natives are a fierce, superstitious Negro race. The
London and Wesleyan Societies have been at work
in the English territory, and continental societies in
the German and Dutch portions.

4. MISSIONS IN OTHER ISLANDS: Other Polynesian groups are the Friendly, the Marquesas, the
Cooks, the Society and other well-known series.
The Friendly or Tonga Islands, like Fiji, have been
won from a state of heathen cannibalism by Wesleyan missionaries; the Marquesas have been evangelized by Hawaiians; Cook's, or Hervey and Society,
by the London Missionary Society. The Church of
England and Wesleyan Societies have done a great
work among the natives of New Zealand, and the
Moravians among the black aborigines of Australia.

The Indian archipelago is largely a Mohammedan
field and has been referred to under that division;
the Philippines, recently ceded to the United States
by Spain, contain a large mixed population, among
which the Roman Catholic Church has been long
at work. These islands are now missionary ground
for American societies and Protestant missionaries
are already on the ground.

CHAPTER XII ·

PROGRESS AT HOME AND ABROAD

WHILE it is to be lamented that the Church is still so inadequately measuring up to the demands and the opportunities of foreign missionary work, it is, on the other hand, most encouraging to compare the conditions as we approach the close of the century with those at its beginning.

The great missionary societies of England started into being during the closing years of the eighteenth century; and it was not until the end of the first decade of the present century that the first foreign missionary society was organized in America; namely, the American Board of Commissioners for Foreign Missions, which dates from 1810. The Missionary Society of the Methodist Episcopal Church followed in 1819, but sent no missionary to a foreign field until nearly one third of the century had gone.

In 1899 the number of missionary societies was 170; including auxiliary societies, about 500; and their income was $15,361,000. There were 5,217 stations where missionaries resided, and about 14,000 out-stations. The number of organized churches was nearly 9,000. There were over 5,000 ordained native preachers. The number of Sunday-schools had grown to about 8,000, with 1,100,000 scholars. The number of communicants in the mission churches is 1,585,000. Dr. James S. Dennis has kindly given the following statistics in regard to the educational work of foreign missions at the close of 1899:

There are 93 universities and colleges, in which there are 33,139 male pupils, and 2,275 female students, making a total of 35,414. There are 358 theological and training schools, in which there are 8,347 male and 3,558 female students; total, 11,905. There are 857 boarding and high schools, having 48,-851 male and 34,297 female students; total, 83,148. Of industrial training institutions and classes there are 134, with 4,622 male and 1,687 female students; total, 6,309. Of medical and nurses' schools and classes there are 63, with 370 male and 219 female students; total, 589. There are 128 kindergartens, with 4,359 pupils. Of village day-schools there are 18,742, with 616,722 boys and 287,720 girls under instruction; total 904,442.

The complete summary of educational institutions and schools of all kinds shows 20,375, in which there are 714,957 male and 331,209 female students; total, 1,046,166.

The Christian Endeavor Society, the Epworth League and other young people's societies are doing very effective work for missions, and are well represented in the foreign fields. The Epworth League of the Methodist Episcopal Church, South, contributed $20,000 to Foreign Missions last year, and there are 45 chapters in the foreign field. The Methodist Episcopal Church has over 80 chapters in China alone.

The first Bible Society was not organized until 1804. This was the British and Foreign Bible Society. The American Bible Society was formed in 1816. Now there are 80 Bible Societies, and they have produced more than 90 entire versions and 250 partial versions, and have circulated, in all, about 360,000,000 copies of the Scriptures.

It was not until 1861 that the first Woman's Foreign Missionary Society was organized in the United States. Now there are 38 in the United States, 9 in Canada, over 30 in Great Britain and the continent of Europe, and a few others in other parts of the world; probably about 80 in all.

Along with this progress there has come naturally a great increase of intelligence. There is much more knowledge of the condition of the great races and the smaller divisions of mankind than formerly. Not only do the missionary periodicals regularly bring to the churches the latest information from all the fields, but the church papers vie with each other in presenting information in regard to the progress and results of missionary labor, and even the secular papers are conveying to their readers many important facts bearing on missionary work.

With increased intelligence there is of course increased interest. In many of the churches missionary zeal is fostered by special meetings at which the different fields are represented, and earnest prayer offered growing out of special needs which have been brought to light.

This increased intelligence and interest are not only manifested in the largely increased offerings, amounting in the Methodist Episcopal and Presbyterian Churches to over a million of dollars annually—including in both cases the amounts contributed by the women's societies—but also in the increasing number of devoted young men and women consecrating themselves to foreign missionary work. In this line the Student Volunteer movement is one of the marked signs of the times. When more than 8,000 young men and women in our seminaries and colleges, including many of the best and brightest students, voluntarily declare to the churches that they are ready to go wherever God may call them in the world-wide field, it certainly indicates a cheering interest in the work on the part of the future leaders of thought in the church.

The recent tour of Mr. John R. Mott in the interest of a federation of Christian students is remarkable, both in showing how heartily the great missionary idea is embraced by students all around the world and also in showing the great progress of Christian missions as evidenced by the fact that in Egypt, in India, in China and Japan, he found hundreds of earnest Christian students ready to join in a world-wide movement of evangelism.

The progress of the work is further emphasized by such contrasts as the following:

Consider Morrison starting out for China in 1807. He is unable to get passage in an English vessel because the East India Company has control of them all and does not wish to encourage the sending of missionaries to China; so that he actually has to come to New York in order to get to his chosen field. Remember that for thirty-five years after that the country was practically closed against missionary labor, and that it was only in 1842 that the treaty ports were opened, and an opportunity given for the entrance of Protestant missions. Bear in mind that for many years after that the entire attitude of the government was unfriendly, and that in many places it was impossible to obtain a foothold. Remember that the Methodist Episcopal Mission, which entered in 1847, had to wait ten years for its first convert, and that other missions had a similar experience.

Over against these facts place the following: The entire empire open to the preaching of Christianity, and protection promised to Christians by imperial proclamation; the mission which waited ten years for its first convert now having over 25,000 communicants; Protestant Christianity with over 80,000 communicants; the Empress Dowager gratefully accepting the elegant copy of the New Testament presented to her on her sixtieth birthday by the Christian women of China; Li Hung Chang, the great Viceroy, visiting foreign countries, and publicly testifying, in New York and elsewhere, his high appreciation of the work of foreign missionaries in his country. In Manchuria, where there was not a single Christian 25 years ago, there were, in 1888, 1,450. In ten years from that date the number had increased ten-fold, and at the end of 1898 was 15,-490; there were 8,875 candidates waiting for baptism, and the contributions of the members amounted to $6,725.

These are simply a few indications of the great progress which has been made, and of the hopeful outlook for the future.

In regard to India, bear in mind the violent opposition of the East India Company to the entrance of Carey and other missionaries; the long history of struggles and difficulties; the attempt to exterminate Christianity by the Sepoy Rebellion in 1857. Then call to mind that the East India Company lowered its flag to half-mast out of respect to Carey when he died, after forty years of faithful labor; that since the Sepoy Rebellion the Methodist Episcopal Mission in North and Northwest India alone has received over 72,000 communicants and that throughout Hindostan there is a widespread spirit of inquiry, and a feeling even among many Hindoos and Mohammedans that Christianity is to be the future religion of the country.

Remember that it was only in 1859 that Japan was opened to the intercourse of foreign nations, and that no open preaching of Christianity was allowed for many years after that date; and now there are 40,000 communicants, with about 300 ordained Japanese ministers. Remember that when the first Parliament of Japan assembled there were 13 Christians in the lower house and that one of them was chosen Speaker; and that the Chief Justice of the Supreme Court has been President of the Young Men's Christian Association in Tokyo.

Remember that the first Protestant missionaries entered Korea in 1884 and that now seven missionary societies are at work there, with over seventy missionaries; that the king sent for Bishop Ninde when he was about to leave the country, in 1895, and in a personal interview asked that many more Christian teachers might be sent to his country; that the present Minister of Education is a graduate of Vanderbilt University, and an earnest Christian, and that Mr. Phil Jaishon, the accomplished editor of the leading newspaper of the country, is a Christian, and an ardent friend of missions and missionaries.

Remember the triumphs of the gospel among various tribes in Africa; the Fiji Islands—barbarous and cannibal at the beginning of the century—so thoroughly Christianized that it would be difficult to find anywhere in the world a community where so large a proportion of the population is to be found at church on every Sabbath day; the Hawaiian Islands, with their large Christian population and their self-supporting churches, sending out missionaries to other islands.

In short, the progress of the work is such as to give the greatest encouragement to all Christian hearts, and to call for our profoundest gratitude. It is also a summons to deeper consecration and to more earnest effort to speedily take the gospel to all mankind.

CHAPTER XIII

THE OUTLOOK

WHEN Adoniram Judson was asked, "What is the prospect of the conversion of Burmah?" his answer was, "It is as bright as the promises of God." That answer could always be made, and was always full of comfort and hope. But foreign missions have long since passed the stage of experiment, the years of faithful seed-sowing and waiting in faith for the harvest. Already the toilers who have gone forth with the precious seed, and have sown it amid many difficulties, "come again with rejoicing, bringing their sheaves with them."

The whole world is practically open to the gospel. The millions of India are under the government of Christian England. The first missionaries there were accustomed to see two funeral pyres built when a man died, one for his dead body and the other for the living body of his widow. She was bound and laid upon the wood, to which fire was applied, that she might go with him in the flames to the other world to minister to him there as she had done here. But the suttee has long since been abolished. Had any one said to Dr. William Butler, when he returned to Bareilly after the ravages of the Sepoy Rebellion to find that the only native

248

Christian had been put to death, that in forty years there would be in that North India field 72,000 communicants and 30,000 adherents, making a Christian army of over 100,000 people, he would have deemed it a wild prophecy. Yet such is the fact to-day, and he lived to see converts coming in at the rate of fifty for every day in the year.

Caste has been a tremendous obstacle to the progress of Christianity in India, but since the schools of Protestant Missions have begun to send up their graduates to the university examinations in Calcutta, and low caste boys and girls have taken the highest prizes over Brahmans in competition with them, caste has lost very much of its importance and is gradually giving way.

In China the haughty exclusion of everything foreign with which the century began first gave place to the opening of treaty ports, and the privilege of travel within thirty miles of them. From this condition of things to the recent proclamation of the Emperor that Christianity is good, teaching men to do to others as they would others should do to them, and declaring toleration for it and protection for its professors throughout the whole Empire, is a long step in the way of progress. When Protestant Missions began their work in China the idea of that nation's sending a minister to a foreign country would not have been suggested as even a remote possibility. Had any one dared to prophesy that before the close of the century she would send a Christian as her ambassador to the United States he would have been deemed beside himself. Yet this has actually taken place. Since the war with Japan there has been an awakening to the need of Western arts and sciences, a demand is made for the study of the English language, and the venerable curriculum of studies for the literary examinations is actually being changed so as to include some of the useful practical knowledge of the times in which we live. The telegraph is already in operation over a large part of the empire and extensive railway lines are soon to be built. Converts are coming into the Church in large numbers, and in some regions whole villages are asking for Christian teachers.

Africa, except a few points along the coast, was practically an unknown continent at the opening of the century. Now about ten millions of square miles, or four fifths of her territory, are under the control of European nations. Mission stations are being rapidly established along her great rivers and on her interior highlands. The "dark continent" is open to the enlightening influences of Christianity.

Japan offers a most inviting field to the efforts of Christendom, and Korea, so long the "Hermit Nation," now seeks the aid of Christian nations to bring to her all the blessings of the most advanced civilization.

In Roman Catholic countries, such as Italy, South America and Mexico, thousands of converts have been gathered within a few years past, and the preaching of an earnest gospel yields results in congregations of people having a conscious experience of salvation through Christ, and ready to endure persecution or to face death itself for their faith.

As has been shown in a previous chapter, to meet the demand created by the opening of the whole world to missionary effort there is no lack of candidates for missionary service. Never before has there been such widespread interest in missionary work in the colleges and seminaries of the land. Never before have so many of the students openly declared themselves as ready and desirous to enter upon work in the foreign field.

While the providential demand is so strong, and the supply of candidates at the same time so large, the money of the world is largely in the hands of Christian people. The wealth of Christian nations is constantly increasing; and a very large share of it is in the hands of members of Christian churches. A Secretary of the Domestic and Foreign Missionary Society of the Protestant Episcopal Church said not long ago that on a certain Sunday he had preached to a church in which there were seven members any one of whom could pay the entire running expenses of that society out of his income and not materially miss the money thus used.

If the wealth of Christian people were only consecrated to God's service in any degree proportionate to the ability of the membership the providential demands of the open field and the supply of earnest laborers at hand would be met by contributions equal to every need. There ought to be a united effort, on the part of Christian ministers and the godly laymen of the churches, to bring the tithes into God's storehouse, so that the great work of evangelization may be pressed to speedy success.

Then, with cordial fellowship and coöperation among the different denominations, the work can be systematically pushed forward to its accomplishment. The growing spirit of unity and mutual helpfulness is a presage of highest encouragement for the future. A more serious purpose to obey the Redeemer's command, and to do it as speedily as possible, is manifesting itself in many portions of the Church.

The work is before us as one that can be done. It is no longer a matter of theory, or one that appeals simply to faith. It is shown to be feasible from a cool, business point of view. The means for its accomplishment are visible, and are at hand. It is time to lay aside all excuses, to arouse the Church from a guilty indifference, to sound from every pulpit God's call to the immediate performance of duty, to send out the best and brightest of our consecrated young men and women, and to follow them with sincere, earnest and unremitting prayer.

In these days, when the faith of our godly fathers and mothers has been surpassed by the actual successes of the work before our eyes, when we stand

PROTESTANT CHURCHES

in the midst of accomplishments far beyond what we
had dared to hope for, when God has shamed the
littleness of our faith by the great blessings poured
out upon the mission fields of the Church, there
should be no whisper of doubt, no hesitation in
instant obedience, but a glad surrender of self and
of the means God has given us, a supreme determination of the Church of God to fulfill the divine
mandate of its Lord, and to usher in the time for
which we pray when we sing:

"Soon may the last glad song arise
Through all the millions of the skies;
That song of triumph which records
That all the earth is now the Lord's."

CHAPTER XIV

STATISTICS

THE statistics of the Methodist Episcopal Foreign Missions which follow are taken from the latest Annual Report—that for 1899. The summaries of 1. The Foreign Missionary Societies of the Evangelical Churches of the United States; 2. The Foreign Missionary Societies of Great Britain and Ireland; 3. The Foreign Missionary Societies of Canada; 4. A General Summary of Protestant Foreign Missions; are those prepared by the Rev. E. E. Strong, D.D.; for the Almanac of Missions, published by the American Board of Foreign Commissioners, at Boston, the use of which he kindly permits and which are prepared with great carefulness and accuracy.

It should be borne in mind that all missions in Protestant countries are excluded from Dr. Strong's tables; and that the amount of income of the Societies includes only that portion of the same that is used for missions outside of Protestant countries, and the sums contributed by the Missions are likewise restricted to missions in non-Protestant lands. It should also be noted that the statistics include the Women's Societies connected with the various Boards.

254

The figures given in the column for self-support in the statistics of the Methodist Episcopal Church include all sums contributed by the native Christians for church building and repairs and current expenses, as well as for the support of the ministry; whereas those given in Dr. Strong's tables are mostly confined to the contributions for pastoral support.

All who have to do with the compilation of statistics realize the great difficulty of securing absolute accuracy. Terms employed are used in such different senses by different Societies, methods of reporting are so various, the inability or neglect of some who furnish reports to fill up all the columns, thus leaving blanks where it is known that there must be figures which ought to be inserted, putting the compiler under the necessity of leaving a blank, or of estimating from the best sources available the amount which should be filled in the blank—all these, and many other things that might be named, make the statistician's pathway a thorny road.

Dr. James S. Dennis is now compiling what will no doubt prove the most accurate summary of all departments of the Foreign Missionary work of Protestant Christendom which has ever been published. It will be published in the forthcoming volumes of the Ecumenical Missionary Conference, which ought to be in possession of every church and every pastor throughout the world.

255

	Foreign Missionarie	Wife of Missionarie	Unmarried Lady Missionarie	Missionarie of the Woman's Foreign Missionary Society	Total Missionarie	Native Ordained Preachers	Native	Native	cal Preachers and their Helpers	Native Workers Woman's Foreign Society	Total Native Workers	Members	Probationers	Total
....	24	18	9	1	52	24	7	16	83	....	125	2,723	546	3,269
....	54	46	5	51	156	137	16²		483	188	1,046	12,175	12,750	24,825
....	75	65	1	76	217	162	654	704	352	505	2,377	32,184	46,420	78,504
....	18	16	1	30	65	60	28	115	88	42	333	3,726	2,183	5,909
....	11	10	..	10	31	...	...	...	10	12	22	556	1,512	2,068
....	11	7	..	4	22	2	13	6	40	19	80	454	246	700
s........	193	162	16	172	543	385	864	912	1,056	7⁶6	3,983	51,818	63,657	115,469

ROMAN CATHOLIC AND

....	1	1	..	2	4	13	1	5	12	7	38	211	26	23
....	2	2	..	4	8	18	16	29	94	2	159	1,656	689	2,345
merica....	11	12	..	7	30	19	44	66	30	34	193	2,520	2,631	5,15
merica....	26	23	16	7	72	28	48	45	42	23	186	2,521	2,058	4,57
ls........	40	38	16	20	114	78	109	145	178	66	576	6,908	5,404	12,31

PROTESTAN

x..........	..	..	..	..	..	19	2	...	43	....	64	3,070	247	3,31
....	..	..	..	..	..	1	2	...	12	....	15	672	250	92
y..........	1	1	..	..	2	117	25	...	425	....	569	13,840	4,375	18,21
....	..	..	..	..	..	45	4	...	2	....	51	5,364	655	6,01
....	..	..	..	..	..	76	19	148	712	....	955	15,558	1,835	17,39
and.......	..	..	..	..	..	44	6	...	74	....	124	7,174	1,129	8,30
ls........	1	1	..	..	2	302	58	148	1,268	....	1,776	45,678	8,491	54

countries	193	162	16	172	543	385	864	912	1,056	766	3,983	51,818	63,657	115
Catholic														
eek	40	38	16	20	114	78	109	145	178	66	576	6,908	5,404	12
nt........	1	1	..	..	2	302	58	148	1,268	....	1,776	45,678	8,491	54
ls........	234	201	32	192	659	765	1,031	1,205	2,502	832	6,335	104,404	77,552	181,9

No. 1.
FOREIGN MISSIONS.

COUNTRIES.

Adults Baptized, 1899	Children Baptized, 1899	Total	Theological Students	High School Pupils	Day School Pupils	Sunday School Scholars	Number of Churches and Chapels	Value	Contributions Missionary Society	Other Benevolences	Self-support
122	161	283	..	....	86	2,880	57	$68,955	$.....	$.....	$2,169
2,322	1,426	3,748	32	770	6,827	14,421	227	155,639	1,143	463	22,493
6,455	5,338	11,793	103	653	19,489	85,785	227	292,579	1,189	4,256	80,353
499	446	945	25	1,051	1,825	8,346	50	53,537	201	271	6,309
354	107	461	..	75	....	1,042	15	7,053	.....	.....	648
65	29	94	..	1,194	1,146	1,246	4	19,100	350	140	41,493
9,817	7,507	17,324	160	3,743	29,373	113,720	580	$596,863	$2,883	$5,130	$153,465

GREEK CHURCH COUNTRIES.

Adults Baptized, 1899	Children Baptized, 1899	Total	Theological Students	High School Pupils	Day School Pupils	Sunday School Scholars	Number of Churches and Chapels	Value	Contributions Missionary Society	Other Benevolences	Self-support
....	33	33	..	52	21	381	8	$18,175	$44	$57	$848
7	60	67	18	174	710	1,102	11	163,300	349	505	15,658
154	239	393	2	231	3,786	2,851	39	67,795	353	665	15,180
92	580	672	11	413	1,655	5,220	32	295,150	630	1,083	69,388
253	912	1,165	31	870	6,172	9,554	90	$544,420	$1,376	$2,810	$101,074

COUNTRIES.

Adults Baptized, 1899	Children Baptized, 1899	Total	Theological Students	High School Pupils	Day School Pupils	Sunday School Scholars	Number of Churches and Chapels	Value	Contributions Missionary Society	Other Benevolences	Self-support
....	153	153	..	...	92	4,448	22	$145,437	$569	$257	$16,597
....	13	13	11	....	....	1,009	5	32,902	393	339	8,780
2	432	434	25	....	....	20,318	127	925,693	1,999	7,837	75,422
6	365	371	5	....	....	6,509	47	190,830	1,099	771	26,397
1	280	281	11	....	....	18,231	122	365,241	4,952	2,179	67,055
....	196	196	..	...	....	18,128	42	333,592	2,087	9,427	49,869
9	1,439	1,448	52	....	92	68,643	365	$1,993,695	$11,099	$20,810	$244,120

MARY.

Adults Baptized, 1899	Children Baptized, 1899	Total	Theological Students	High School Pupils	Day School Pupils	Sunday School Scholars	Number of Churches and Chapels	Value	Contributions Missionary Society	Other Benevolences	Self-support
9,817	7,507	17,324	160	3,743	29,373	113,720	580	$596,863	$2,883	$5,130	$153,465
253	912	1,165	31	870	6,172	9,554	90	544,420	1,376	2,810	101,074
9	1,439	1,448	52	....	92	68,643	365	1,993,695	11,099	20,810	244,120
10,079	9,858	19,937	243	4,613	35,637	191,917	1,035	$3,134,978	$15,358	$28,750	$498,659

(17)

Foreign Missionary Societies of the Evangelical Churches of the United States, 1898–99.

SOCIETIES.	Date of Organization.	Principal Stations.	Out-stations.	American Missionaries Male.	American Missionaries Female.	Native Laborers.	Churches.	Communicants.	Added last year.	Under instruction.	Native Contributions in Dollars.	Total Income in Dollars.
American Board	1810	100	1,326	186	343	3,155	492	49,782	5,047	60,780	$135,987	$644,200
Presbyterian Board (North)	1837	111	1,081	283	419	2,030	368	35,995	4,844	21,516	5,446	863,403
Presbyterian Board (South)	1861	40	176	68	91	92	36	3,378	484	397	9,987	145,000
Reformed Church in America (Dutch)	1832	23	225	35	55	448	42	4,453	399	7,231	21,216	126,838
United Presbyterian Board	1859	20	270	40	72	638	65	7,925	573	31,290		138,982
Reformed Presbyterian Church (Covenanter)	1856	5	9	10	15	35	3	293	61	645	2,617	27,351
Cumberland Presbyterian Church	1878	6	7	11	16	25	10	800	100	200	300	20,000
Reformed Church of the U. S. (German)	1873	3	56	7	9	33	15	1,817	254			30,170
Reformed Presby. Gen'l Synod (Covenanter)	1836	8		2	8	45	11	1,150	80	370		6,400
German Evangelical Synod of No. America.	1869	4	6	7	5	38	4	807	176	1,506	10,000	17,000
Associate Reformed Synod of the South	1874	3	11	3	6	7	10	281	39		559	8,792
American Baptist Missionary Union	1814	91	1,495	182	277	4,020	1,028	128,294	7,575	31,254	118,583	563,494
Baptist Convention, Southern	1845	100	140	35	47	128	100	5,347	845	2,446	7,110	109,267
Free Baptists	1833	7	6	8	16	75	12	797	62	3,208	390	20,110
Seventh-Day Baptists	1847	1	1	1	3	10	1	51	11	165	600	3,500
German Baptist Brethren (Tunkers)	1884	11	6	4	4	17	11	238	37			7,890
Methodist Episcopal Church	1819	134	500	235	431	4,403	676	124,611	5,520	49,919	249,939	954,063
Methodist Episcopal Church, South	1845	56		74	59	234	102	9,503	462	1,483	13,403	220,495
Methodist Protestant Church	1888	8	19	5	9	26	6	326	71	43	235	10,996
Free Methodist Church	1882	5	9	4	8	13	2	99	25	281	100	12,932
Wesleyan Methodist	1890	1	1	4	7	5	1	24				7,000
Protestant Episcopal Church	1835	200		47	41	403	45	5,582	390	20	9,219	235,029
Evangelical Association	1876	1	21	2	8	32	18	890	85	4,534	1,050	8,500
United Brethren in Christ	1853	11	75	20	8	13	40	4,286	149	1,159	3,730	65,000
Evangelical Lutheran, General Synod	1841	6	8	12	15	462	423	6,516	1,210	6,451	7,695	48,508
Evangelical Lutheran, General Council	1845	7	191	7	10	160	5	2,002		2,719		19,378
United Synod of Evangelical Lutheran Church in the South	1893			2	2			60				4,000
Foreign Christian Miss'y Society (Disciples)	1875	1	39	50	45	6	3	5,280	1,020	150	8,008	144,783
Christian Church (Convention)	1886	75	25	2	3	101	91	332	65	1,570	218	6,673
American Bible Society	1816	2		21	12	15	7			594		152,696
American Tract Society	1825		40	2		243						1,677
American Friends	1871	19	24	14	39	84	23	1,290	106	1,456	2,183	38,336
Woman's Union Missionary Society	1860	8			18	304		298		6,100		47,967
Totals		1,067	5,776	1,383	2,095	17,300	3,650	402,507	29,690	237,487	$608,575	$4,710,430

NAME OF SOCIETY.	Stations	Out-stations	Men	Women	Total Native Helpers	Communicants	Added last year	Pupils Under Instruction	Income in Great Britain
Baptist Missionary Society	807	**	164	114	403	†19,269	†1,790	14,669	$376,657
Baptist Zenana Society	24	**		68	220			3,565	49,605
China Inland Mission	164	169	331	481	605	8,176	1,029	1,726	267,303
Church Missionary Society	520	*	530	383	6,154	64,904	493	88,094	1,899,135
Church of England Zenana Missionary Society	72			221	850			10,468	230,575
Church of Scotland	21	77	44	85	537	2,334	251	5,957	188,035
Women's Association									71,624
Free Church of Scotland	45	304	127	135	1,149	10,977	395	35,298	254,570
Women's Society									79,860
Friends' Foreign Missionary Association	14	232	31	47	1,035	2,730		20,869	106,315
London Missionary Society	97	1,260	196	226	5,240	52,803	1,817	50,613	666,526
Methodist New Connexion	197	*	8	6	78	2,527	523	555	27,051
Moravian Missions	137	45	186	186	297	33,505	204	24,425	‡145,000
North African Mission	17	*	30	72	15			500	54,600
Presbyterian Church of England	75	120	35	49	156	5,943	477	5,825	117,985
Presbyterian Church of Ireland	19	83	32	34	385	1,960	490		101,344
Primitive Methodist	10	25	13	8	16	1,456			41,029
"Regions Beyond" Missionary Union§	9	4	33	19	15	200		500	52,532
Society for Propagation of the Gospel	500	4,000	611	170	3,326	‖70,000		38,000	661,775
South American Missionary Society	24	21	38	20	6				41,793
United Methodist Free Churches	109	90	18	10	16	11,098		8,663	61,170
United Presbyterian Free Church	114	268	93	43	881	26,971	3,567	21,070	305,186
Universities' Mission to Central Africa	36	*	94	36	118	1,115		3,245	174,950
Welsh Calvinistic Meth. (or Welsh Presbyterian)	15	235	20	20	56	3,642	620	5,945	37,070
Wesleyan Missionary Society	276	320	182		180	46,262	1,622	90,117	557,901
Women's Auxiliary	44	300		52	140			18,254	66,927
Zenana Bible and Medical Mission	24	12		92	313	6,323			99,863
Totals	**3,370**	**7,565**	**2,816**	**2,577**	**22,191**	**372,195**	**13,278**	**448,362**	**$6,689,191**

In addition to the above there are many other organizations in Great Britain working for Foreign Missions, wholly or in part, the expenditures of which for this branch of Christian effort are estimated as:

17 Other Societies.............. $247,976   12 Missions to the Jews.............. $407,112

3 Medical Missions.............. 17,217

7 Tract and Bible Societies...... 405,244   Total.............. $1,077,549

This makes the grand total income of British Foreign Missionary and kindred societies $7,766,740.

    Total.............. $7,766,740.

* Included in first column.   † Less than normal, owing largely to disastrous floods in Shantung, North China.
‡ Excluding contributions from America.   § Embraces Congo Balolo Mission, Peruvian and Argentine Missions.
‖ An approximation.

TABLE No. 4.

FOREIGN MISSIONARY SOCIETIES IN CANADA.

SOCIETIES.	Stations.	Out-stations.	American Laborers.			Native Laborers.	Churches.	Communicants.	Added last year.	Native Contributions in Dollars.	Contributions in Canada.
			Men.	Women.	Total.						
Congregational Foreign Missionary Society	2	..	3	4	7	6	1	43	9	$10	$4,500
Baptist Convention, Maritime Provinces	7	9	8	11	19	48	7	314	59	243	15,306
Baptist Foreign Missionary Board of Ontario and Quebec	10	75	10	18	28	190	33	3,886	347	1,200	31,807
Missionary Society Methodist Church	99	31	137	82	219	64	..	5,762	213	3,005	262,974
Presbyterian Board of Missions	98	120	40	70	110	290	..	3,493	458	11,984	175,222
Church of England	3	10	4	2	6	15	1	..	..	....	16,320
Totals	219	245	202	187	389	613	42	13,498	1,086	$16,442	$506,129

INDEX

INDEX

Beirut, Jewish missions in, 108.
Benevolent agencies not missionary work, 24, 28.
Bengal, Work in, 94, 109.
Berbers, Work among the, 114.
Berlin Missionary Society, 131.
Berlin Training School for Missionaries, 129.
Berlin Women's Verein, 141.
Best kind of preaching, 66.
Bethel Ship, The, 178.
Bethlehem, Pa., Missionaries in, 133.
Bible distribution in Suabia, 116.
Bible Societies in Europe, 116.
Bible translations in Carey's time, 91.
Birthplace of American Missions, 146.
Bishop of Japan, The first, 199.
Blodget, Dr., at Shanghai Conference, 74.
Blythewood, North Kaffir Mission at, 119.
Board of Missions of the Methodist Episcopal Church, South, 196.
Boardman, George Dana, 159.
Bogue, Dr. David, Address of, in the *Evangelical Magazine*, 97.
Bombay, 95, 107, 117, 148, 152.
Boone, J. W., Protestant Episcopal Missionary Bishop, 199.
Boresen among the Santhals, 142.
Borneo, 95, 181.
Bowen, Rev. J. W., in Brazil, 195.
Brahman converts, 107.
Brainerd, David, 47, 184.
Brazil, Missions to, 81, 190, 198.
Breklum Society, The, 141.
Bridgman, Elijah C., called to mission work, 48.
British and Foreign Bible Society, 116.
British Colonies, Missionaries to, 101.

British East India Company, 148.
British Guiana, Mission to, 99.
Bruce, Rev. John, 119.
Buenos Ayres, 167.
Bulgaria, 178.
Burden, of Church Missionary Society, 102.
Burma entered, 95.
Burmese, First Baptist mission to, 158.
Burns, Missionary Bishop for Africa, 167.
Burns, Rev. Wm. C., in China, 105.
Burt, Rev. William, D.D., 179.
Butler, Dr. William, 174, 176, 248.
Butler, J. W., 177.

Calabar (Kingston), College at, 92.
Calcutta, 41, 94, 107, 117.
Call to missionary work, 44.
Call to the ministry, 42.
Calvinistic Methodists, 109.
Calvinistic Presbyterians, 109.
Cambridge University Volunteers, The, 95.
Cameroon, Africa, 129.
Canada, 108, 110.
Canadian Foreign Missionary Societies, 206.
Canton, Mr. Burns in, 105.
Cape Colony, 132, 136.
Cape Maclean, 120.
Carey, William, 87, 88, 89.
Carrow, Rev. Goldsmith, 168.
Carter, Dr. Thomas, 177.
Caste giving way, 249.
"Castle and Falcon," The, 97, 101.
Cawnpore and Delhi, 94.
Celebes, The, 144.
Central America, 135.
Central Mexico Mission Conference, 197.
Ceylon, Mission in, 91.
Ceylonese, Work among the, 152.
Chapin, Miss J. M., 169.

262

INDEX

264

INDEX

INDEX

INDEX

INDEX

INDEX

Lightning Source UK Ltd.
Milton Keynes UK
UKHW022019090119

335262UK00010B/699/P